Communications
in Computer and Information Science   680

Commenced Publication in 2007
Founding and Former Series Editors:
Alfredo Cuzzocrea, Dominik Ślęzak, and Xiaokang Yang

More information about this series at http://www.springer.com/series/7899

Tiago Silva da Silva
Bernardo Estácio · Josiane Kroll
Rafaela Mantovani Fontana (Eds.)

Agile Methods

7th Brazilian Workshop, WBMA 2016
Curitiba, Brazil, November 7–9, 2016
Revised Selected Papers

 Springer

Editors
Tiago Silva da Silva
Universidade Federal de São Paulo
São José dos Campos
Brazil

Bernardo Estácio
Pontifícia Universidade Católica do Rio
  Grande do Sul
Porto Alegre
Brazil

Josiane Kroll
Pontifícia Universidade Católica do Rio
  Grande do Sul
Porto Alegre
Brazil

Rafaela Mantovani Fontana
Universidade Federal do Paraná
Curitiba
Brazil

ISSN 1865-0929   ISSN 1865-0937 (electronic)
Communications in Computer and Information Science
ISBN 978-3-319-55906-3   ISBN 978-3-319-55907-0 (eBook)
DOI 10.1007/978-3-319-55907-0

Library of Congress Control Number: 2017935845

Printed on acid-free paper

This Springer imprint is published by Springer Nature
The registered company is Springer International Publishing AG
The registered company address is: Gewerbestrasse 11, 6330 Cham, Switzerland

Preface

The 7th Brazilian Workshop on Agile Methods (WBMA 2016) was held during November 7–9, 2016, in Curitiba, Brazil. The workshop is the research track in the Agile Brazil conference. WBMA is an academic event that focuses on agile software development.

This year's edition comes with a history of success. Our past editions received an impressive number of both paper submissions and attendees (students, researchers, and practitioners) from different countries. We repeated the success this year and influenced even more academic integration in an industrial context. We believe this integration create ideas, opportunities, and innovations for all involved.

We received 35 submissions (40% of acceptance rate). All the accepted papers were peer reviewed by three referees and evaluated on the basis of technical quality, relevance, significance, and clarity. The Organizing Committee decided to accept ten full papers and four short papers. Accepted papers in this edition present empirical results and literature reviews on: agile implementation in government and distributed environments; design thinking and projects inception; testing and technical debt; motivation and gamification; training, modeling, and project management; maturity models; and quality assurance. In order to improve the quality of papers and reviews, the Organizing Committee offered two prizes in this edition: best paper and best reviewer awards.

This CCIS volume comprises peer-reviewed versions of ten full papers and four short papers.

The organizers thank the Program Committee members for their contributions, and would especially like to thank all those who submitted papers, even though only a fraction could be accepted. We also thank Springer for producing these high-quality proceedings of WBMA 2016.

November 2016

Josiane Kroll
Rafaela Mantovani Fontana
Tiago Silva da Silva
Bernardo Estácio

Organization

WBMA 2016 was organized by the Federal University of Paraná (UFPR), Federal University of São Paulo (UNIFESP), and Pontifical University Catholic of Rio Grande do Sul (PUCRS) and it was supported by the Araucaria Foundation and CNPq (National Council for Scientific and Technological Development) in cooperation with Springer.

Executive Committee

Conference Chair

Josiane Kroll   PUCRS, Brazil
Rafaela Mantovani Fontana   UFPR, Brazil

Program Chair

Tiago Silva da Silva   UNIFESP, Brazil
Bernardo Estácio   PUCRS, Brazil

Program Committee

Conference Chair

Josiane Kroll   PUCRS, Brazil
Rafaela Mantovani Fontana   UFPR, Brazil

Program Chair

Tiago Silva da Silva   UNIFESP, Brazil
Bernardo Estácio   PUCRS, Brazil

Additional Reviewers

Adolfo Neto
Alan Santos
Alexandre Vasconcelos
Alfredo Goldman
Bernardo Estácio
Eduardo Guerra
Elder de Macedo
  Rodrigues
Fabio Kon
Fábio Levy Siqueira

Filipe Correia
Graziela Tonin
Hugo Sereno Ferreira
Josiane Kroll
Jutta Eckstein
Luciana Zaina
Maarit Laanti
Maria Istela Cagnin
Maurício Aniche
Patrícia Vilain

Paulo Meirelles
Rafael Prikladnicki
Rafaela Mantovani
  Fontana
Ricardo Britto
Rodrigo de Toledo
Tiago Silva da Silva
Vinicius Garcia
Viviane Santos
Xiaofeng Wang

Sponsoring Institutions

Araucária Foundation (Fundação Araucária)
CNPq - National Council for Scientific and Technological Development (Conselho Nacional de Pesquisa e Desenvolvimento Científico e Tecnolgógico)

Contents

Short Papers

Full Papers

An Empirical Study on the Adoption of Agile Software Development in Public Organizations

Isaque Vacari[1(✉)] and Rafael Prikladnicki[2]

[1] Free Software Laboratory, Embrapa Agricultural Informatics, Campinas, SP, Brazil
isaque.vacari@embrapa.br
[2] Computer Science School, Pontifical Catholic University of Rio Grande do Sul,
Porto Alegre, RS, Brazil
rafaelp@pucrs.br

Abstract. The government has been adopting agile software development in order to improve the results of their IT projects. However, there is a lack of structured information about its adoption in this context. Since the public sector have undergone a significant process of modernization to improve the quality of public service, the goal of this study is to report from an empirical study, provide information that may enhance the understanding of the implications of adopting agile software development within public organizations, proposing a set of recommendations for its adoption.

Keywords: Empirical software engineering · Agile software development · Agile methodologies · Agile methods · Public organizations · Public sector · Government

1 Introduction

In the context of software-producing companies, agility and innovation have become slogans. The point is not just to create new products or to significantly improve existing products. It is to do this quickly, before competitors take up space. This reality drives them to be agile and to actively involve their customers in the software development process. In this direction, agile software development (ASD) have played a key role in the development of a modern production process by adding value to the product to the customer in the shortest possible time. In addition, ASD have become an important research topic [1] arousing the gradual interest of organizations (public and private) [2,3].

However, despite the increasing number of studies in this area in recent years, there is a lack of structured information on the adoption of these methods in the public sector. Thus, since public organizations (POs) are the part of the economy responsible for providing services to society by improving the quality of life of its citizens, software has become a vital component for the government to integrate, in an innovative way, the needs of society to its administrative capacity, and technique of performing public services [4], it was defined that the

© Springer International Publishing AG 2017
T. Silva da Silva et al. (Eds.): WBMA 2016, CCIS 680, pp. 3–15, 2017.
DOI: 10.1007/978-3-319-55907-0_1

general objective of this research as being "to present, from an empirical study, information that can improve the understanding of the implications of adopting of ASD from the perspective of public organizations, proposing a set of recommendations for its adoption". In the sequence, the work motivation is explained, characterizing the relevance of the theme and the main research challenges, its relevant results and its contributions, as well as the used methodology in this research.

2 Background and Related Work

A study of the Standish Group [5] with 3.555 Information Technology (IT) projects of the United States government in the last 10 years (2003–2012) revealed that only 6% of them were successful, such as those finalized on time; within the budget and which included all the features originally specified. Another 52% were considered challenging, such as those who used a larger-than-expected budget, finalized late and did not include all the functionality originally specified. Lastly, 42% have completely failed, such as those canceled at some point in the software life cycle.

In Brazil, audits carried out in various government agencies and entities revealed that although the information systems of these organizations effectively contribute to the activities of the business areas, the high rate of discontent over time to meet the demands of systems is a concern and indicates that organizations want greater agility in the delivery of this service [6]. In addition, studies have reported the lack of clear evidence on the positive impacts of IT in this sector, since, in many cases, IT systems do not present real benefits, only exaggerated and unrealistic expectations [7].

In order to overcome this history of software project failures in the public sector, some supervisory bodies from the United States of America (USA), the United Kingdom (UK) and Brazil issued a favorable opinion on the adoption of agile methods in government IT projects [8–11], supporting an agile culture throughout the public sector where the development of long-term software solutions with deliveries only at the end of the project is not allowed without demonstrating real benefits during their execution.

Even with this favorable opinion, the adoption of agile methods in the public sector has faced some challenges. Agile methods are incompatible with the hierarchical and bureaucratic structures common to POs [12]. Many POs, especially large ones, have spent years modifying their culture so that software development processes are defined and followed, and it is difficult to make a change to a work model in which processes are adaptive and defined by the team itself [13]. Although it is possible to contract agile software development in a way that guarantees, contractor (government) and contracted (provider), the adoption of some agile practices; it is to be expected, tough, that they are supplemented with prescriptive features and as a consequence it can begin to lose some of its agility [14].

In Brazil, state bureaucracy and the legal and normative framework have hampered the work of POs to implement governance and management models that are more agile and compatible with the dynamics of the contemporary world [15]. Saraiva's study [15] revealed that the bureaucratic logic of POs is responsible for a complex dynamic between employees and the organization. The notion of bureaucracy is so ingrained that it refers to the idea of immobility, since innovative precepts to carry out the work are ignored or do not go forward, such as the strength of the current regulatory approaches. In general terms, the research has shown that POs are faced with the need for modernity, but there is a widespread fear of the new – distinct from what is established in existing norms and manuals – which make them give up any transformation remaining as they are, as well as accentuate the ignorance of employees regarding their own potential for development and the fear of working in a flexible context without the presence of the manual that provides and regulates everything.

Overall, even with all these problems and challenges, studies on the adoption of agile methods in the public sector have shown that they have led POs to achieve better results than those that would be possible to achieve with traditional approaches [13]. Thus, since the nuances of adopting agile methods in POs are not widely known and observe how this is reflected in the scope of government, it is a valuable exercise for scientific research to understand and broaden knowledge in this area.

3 Research Methodology

The elaboration of the set of recommendations for the adoption of agile software development in POs originated from a research methodology organized in four phases. The first phase of "theoretical reference" (F1) is based and detailed mainly in a secondary study of the systematic literature review (LSR) on the subject, published in the International Conference on Software Engineering and Knowledge Engineering (SEKE) [16].

The second phase of "empirical study" (F2) is based on a qualitative research approach, through a case study [17]. Regarding the delimitation of the units of analysis, four software development teams (totaling eighteen subjects) were selected and interviewed – two large and medium-sized Brazilian POs, which provide IT solutions for the Public Administration and the agricultural sector, both with experience in the application of ASD in government. The data collection instruments used in the research were: semi-structured interviews and content analysis. The interviews were recorded electronically in audio (with the consent of the interviewees) and transcribed for future reference. For the treatment and analysis of data, the technique of Bardin was used [18].

In phase 3 (F3), we sought to consolidate the results achieved in phases F1 and F2, forming a framework of theoretical and empirical results. The last phase (F4) consisted of the elaboration and consolidation of the set of recommendations for adoption of ASD in POs. It is worth noting that a preliminary set of recommendations has been drawn up. Subsequently, new interviews with specialists were conducted aiming at some degree of stability in the final set of recommendations.

4   Case Studies

Considering that the research undertaken wants to understand how software is developed within a public organization, it is evidenced that the object of study is circumscribed within the scope of the human and social sciences and that a research with this character directs to the use of a qualitative research method, because what is sought are answers that indicate the real state of the delimited object unraveling as it occurs from the subjects who exercise it. Among the various qualitative research alternatives, the case study was chosen because it is based, as Yin points out [17], in the identification of answers to questions in which the research problem consists in seeking the "how" and the "why", as well as in the focus of complex contemporary events with real life context and in the effort to maintain the universal characteristics of the studied context. The government offers a context full of complexities, dramas and ambiguities. Capturing this combination of elements is the advantage of case studies, whether for practice knowledge or for the study [19].

4.1   The Selection of Public Organizations

This research began with a differentiated sample, with two POs, covering Embrapa Agricultural Informatics (CNPTIA) and the *Cia. de Processamento de Dados do Grande do Sul* (in Portuguese) (PROCERGS) because different conditions were assumed to exist in the context of governments that affect software development in POs. The choice of these two POs was made, firstly, for purely organizational reasons, referring to the availability of financial resources, the time available, the opportunity to access the object of interest (software projects with agile methods) and the possibility of recruiting subjects for the study.

4.2   The Selection of Research Subjects

From agile software development projects carried out at POs – as a starting point for the identification of data collection strategies – the selection of the subjects that composed the research was carried out in function of two focus areas defined in this research as analysis dimension. The organizational dimension is the first one. It raised, along with managers, relevant institutional aspects about the organizational culture. It is assumed that organizational culture influences, promotes, facilitates, hampers, favors and/or makes the adoption of agile methods with greater or lesser acceptability in the organization [12]. While the project dimension focused on the members' perception of how they understand teamwork, alignment with business objectives, and the execution of software development processes and practices; however, was interested in knowing how agile software development happens and develops within the projects. Considering the definition of the chosen dimensions and also the professional experience of the researchers, we opted for the quantities of subjects per sample size given in Table 1.

Table 1. Quantitative research subjects by POs and dimension

Public organization	Dimension	Subjects
CNPTIA	Organizational	1 Assessor
	Project 1 (CaS01)	2 Developers; 1 Project Manager
	Project 2 (CaS02)	1 Project Manager; 1 Developer
	Total	**6 subjects**
PROCERGS	Organizational	1 Manager
	Project 3 (CaS03)	1 Product Owner; 1 Systems Analyst;
		1 Scrum Master/Developer;
		1 Quality Assurance; 2 Developers
	Project 4 (CaS04)	1 Systems Analyst;
		1 Scrum Master/Developer;
		2 Developers; 1 Quality Assurance
	Total	**12 subjects**

4.3 The Data Collection Instruments

In the scope of data collection instruments, this research is based on the use of two techniques: (1) interviews and (2) analysis of documents. It is worth mentioning that the adoption of observation as a data collection instrument became unfeasible because the projects of CNPTIA and PROCERGS are in networks and, often, inter-institutional or interdepartmental, which prevents the participation of other people as observers. Apart from these facts, the observation would require an immersion in the environment where the events happen, which is difficult to accept on the part of the subjects and the selected organizations.

Since software development is performed by people, it was realized that the question of research would only be understood if it incorporated the experience of the individuals who inhabit the physical space circumscribed in the analyzed case studies. This fact alone justifies the option of the interview as an instrument of data collection. Among the various types of interviews, the individual interview was chosen, following a semi-structured interview protocol. The analysis of documents was the second instrument of data collection on which this research was based in order to guarantee the validity of the results. The types of documents reviewed covered the Company Master Plan, Product Vision Document, Product Backlog and Project Reports.

4.4 The Treatment and Analysis of Data

The treatment and data analysis of this research was inspired by the proposal of Bardin [18], which predicts three fundamental phases: (1) pre-analysis, (2) exploration of the material and (3) treatment of results – inference and interpretation. The Pre-analysis included the conversion of the audio from the interviews into text in the document "Text of the Interviews". It also helped to define the topics to be addressed, and in some categories information summaries were organized, including information about the project, the team, the customer and business relationship, the process and practices, knowledge and experience of subjects.

It is worth mentioning that these categories were derived mainly from the theoretical reference and a single category was created after the data collection (the knowledge and experience of the subjects). In addition, although the main instrument of data collection was the semi-structured interview, the complete analysis was not limited to the data coming from this single instrument, but also used internal and external documents to the project, previously mentioned.

4.5 Consolidation of Empirical Results

The four case studies carried out evidenced several aspects of Software Engineering (SE) and ASD, some of them being presented in the sequence. A common feature found was the execution time of the projects that takes place over several years, which can increase the costs for their execution. But with agile methods, software deliveries happen earlier – weekly or monthly – with deployments in production in months instead of years. So the benefits of an IT solution can return to their "investors" as early as possible. In addition, it was found that the projects were able to experiment and evaluate the practices and technologies necessary for their development.

In PROCERGS, there was little individual space and more collective space and everything close to software development, which requires a daily exercise of the essence of self-organization. On the other hand, CNPTIA found more individual space and less collective space and distant people, which requires the help of tools, emails and telephones for communication. The challenge in these environments, albeit with different approaches, is to learn how to work together, such as ensuring that people will be available at the time they are asked for. However, it was found that a great inhibitor of teamwork is the allocation of people concomitantly in several projects (CaS01) (CaS02).

Knowledge and experience in project management were found to be critical, which should not be a new discovery. In projects (CaS01) (CaS02), this aspect of the SE was shared among some people in the team (Product Owner, Systems Analyst, Quality Analyst and Scrum Master), which illustrates an example of responsibility shared by the team instead of specific people, complemented with some organizational skills, including mentoring services and training programs. While in the projects (CaS03) (CaS04), the specific role of the project manager is still mandatory in the formulation, approval and execution of the project, however during its execution a shared commitment was observed in relation to the accomplishment of the objectives that the team would accept.

With respect to alignment with business objectives, the four projects studied presented a new business solution rather than just the provision of a software product. In these cases, the management of the organizational impacts resulting from the business changes were managed from the beginning of the project. They have formed committees or groups – made up of clients, user representatives, and some projects with IT people – to provide guidance and direction to achieve common goals and not to restrain team initiatives. This project governance strategy proved to be adequate for effective acceptance of the software product in the organization. However, it requires committees or groups to actively participate in the process of developing and solving organizational problems, as well as representing the interests of system users.

With regard to the project follow-up, two projects (CaS03) (CaS04) presented evidence of how a well-done burndown chart offers the real perception of how much work in progress will be completed by the due date or not. The strategy adopted in both teams consisted in reestimating the remaining time to completion of the tasks daily, which made the burndown graph more precise. These teams reported using visual management tools in the form of a kanban framework for project tracking as well. They have pointed to daily meetings as important to assist in the follow-up of the project, such as review meetings with the client to assess whether the project is headed in the right direction. On the other hand, project teams (CaS01) (CaS02) found it difficult to establish a routine of daily meetings with the developers because of their participation in other projects simultaneously. The monitoring of the project was carried out based on information contained in electronic spreadsheets (CaS01) and tools to support the software development process (CaS02).

Regarding software development, the four projects presented evidence of using the iterative and incremental approach, establishing well-defined feedback cycles, adjusting the software to create an optimal interpretation of the product. In addition, three projects (CaS02) (CaS03) (CaS04) preferred to incorporate aspects of software testing at the beginning and during iterations rather than leaving them to the end. Two projects (CaS03) (CaS04) stated that they were practicing the creation of test scenarios based on the Behavior Driven Development (BDD) technique with the support of the quality analyst, but evidences of the writing of unit tests and automation of tests were not found for these two projects. On the other hand, the project (CaS02) presented evidences in the creation and execution of automated tests, covering unit tests and functional tests; In addition, this team presented good knowledge in code integration and software release in production in an automated way. Lastly, none of the projects studied presented evidence of the use of Test Driven Development (TDD).

With regard to environments and tools to support software development, all teams reported the importance of having specific environments for the project, including development environment, testing, certification, training and production. The teams (CaS03) (CaS04) reported difficulties in obtaining real data to carry out their work, since many of them are confidential and can not be made available to the team. The teams reported the use of tools to support software development, preferably open source. The team (CaS01) has adopted a content management tool to share information with all members of the project, since they are distributed in various regions of Brazil. The same team pointed out the importance of using other forms of communication when customers and users are dispersed geographically, including video conferencing, email and telephone equipment. Finally, no personal characteristics of multidisciplinarity were found, on the contrary, managers, architects, analysts, developers, interface designers and testers are still a reality.

Regarding the reasons for the adoption of agile methods, CNPTIA was the protagonist in the adoption of agile methods in government with the use of Extreme Programming (XP) in an important project in the early 2000s. Its use was motivated as a response to failure of an earlier project. The success of the project motivated its protagonists to disseminate the principles and practices of XP to other people, some of them being adopted in some subsequent projects with some positive results. However, the adoption of XP and any other method of software development is not complete and unanimous in the Company. In PROCERGS, the adoption of agile methods began in 2012, that is, well after its experimentation and evaluation by the private sector. Although it started later, the use of agile software development is virtually complete in the Company. Its use was motivated by a restructuring that aimed to make the Company more efficient and less bureaucratic. Currently, PROCERGS is a good reference in the adoption of agile methods in POs, mainly for state companies and public IT companies.

With respect to the benefits, the four studies show evidence that agile software development based on short value deliveries contributes to customers remaining enthusiastic and committed to project results through to the end, which increases trust and confidence. Satisfaction with the work performed and with the system developed. In addition, there seems to be a new fact, although software projects in POs are still of long duration, delivery in increments of value to the client, as well as the deployment of software in smaller periods of time creates greater capacity of acceptance of the system in the company, being more resistant to the eventual administrative and political changes, typical of government.

Regarding the challenges, according to the information collected, it can be said that the difficulties of the agile development in CNPTIA are centered in the allocation of people to work in several projects at the same time, in the difficulty of the top management in determining its use in an institutional way, in the difficulty of sharing knowledge and information among people, in the lack of training allied to coaching in loco and in the different types of existing systems. Although there are several proposals for applicable solutions to minimize problems in adopting agile methods in POs, some alternatives have been found in PROCERGS, including: senior management commitment in contracting training and specific coaching in product management practices; training teams with full time dedication to software development preferably with people who know each other the longest.

With regard to the formation of an agile culture in the organization, according to the information collected, both companies perceived external opportunities and absorbed the use of agile methods in pilot projects with people willing to try the new one, being supported by the top management. From there, its positive experiences were refined and expanded to other projects within the company.

This means that agile culture was born in these two organizations from the experimentation of the object of study in subcultures. Thus, it can be inferred that POs learn and modify themselves.

PROCERGS is seeking to advance in the adoption of ASD practices and knowledge sharing strategies among teams. On the other hand, CNPTIA has not been able to establish new advances remaining as it is, including with some difficulties in the formation of teams and in the sharing of experiences among the people. For this reason, agile methods are not perceived as a finished process that is finalized when a particular achievement is achieved. Contrariwise, agile methods is something that is continuously processed and depends on a set of factors linked to the people and the environment where it is inserted to achieve new and better results continuously. This signals to the interactive, continuous and dynamic character of the agile methods abstracted from the case studies carried out.

5   Results

As previously mentioned, this research proposes to consolidate the information found, in theory (through LSR [16]) and in practice (through the case studies), on the adoption of agile methods in POs in a framework, proposing a set of recommendations for its adoption in the context of the public sector. One of the biggest reasons for adopting agile methods is the benefits they can bring to the POs, which are seen as a response to the history of failures of IT projects in government. In relation to the benefits achieved in the adoption of agile methods in POs, the following aspects were identified, according to Table 2.

In some cases, the very optimistic image in the theoretical level of agile methods can be countered by a practical reality dominated by challenges, difficulties and concrete problems. With respect to the problems and challenges faced, the following aspects were identified, as shown in Table 3.

5.1   For Beyond Results ... A Set of Recommendations

The theoretical and empirical studies showed evidence of the adoption of agile software development in POs. Such methods are known and can be tried and repeated in the context of government. However, what presents as a challenge are the issues of change management that emerge from a new way of doing the work and find a path of small initial successes for its expansion as a development method commonly accepted and used in POs.

In this sense, the analysis suggests that a good alternative is to start adoption with people willing to change strongly supported by senior management, working on important pilot projects in a more open and team-friendly environment. Then the change will depend on the expansion and interaction with other teams aimed at reaching the great majority of the organization. Throughout the adoption process, people should form an ecosystem of learning and continuous improvement not to accommodate themselves with the first achievements and

Table 2. Benefits achieved in the adoption of agile methods in POs

Perspective	Aspect	Sources
Humane	Improved alignment and collaboration between IT and business	(LSR) (CaS01) (CaS02) (CaS03) (CaS04)
	Increased team morale and reduced reliance on contractors	(LSR)
	Communication improvement	(LSR) (CaS03) (CaS04)
	Improvement in teamwork and holistic vision of the project	(CaS03) (CaS04)
Organizational	Earlier delivery of value to the customer	(LSR) (CaS02) (CaS03) (CaS04)
	Increase in customer satisfaction	(LSR) (CaS02) (CaS03)
	Improved project visibility	(LSR)
	Reduction of costs	(LSR)
	Improved ability to manage changes and priorities	(LSR) (CaS01) (CaS02)
Technical	Improvement in learning new technologies	(LSR) (CaS02)
	Improvement in product quality and code	(LSR)
	Increased productivity of teams	(LSR)

the comfort zone, that is, to improve always, not just once. From this reasoning, the final set of recommendations proposed was divided into three phases: (1) Preparation, (2) Implementation and (3) Learning.

(1) Preparation: In the preparation phase, the theoretical and empirical studies have signaled five recommendations that need to be duly considered before beginning the adoption of agile methods. First, people need to be considered in change strategies. Second, there must be people who are receptive to change. Third, management's commitment to this effort is extremely important. Fourth, the criticality and importance of pilot projects need to be carefully considered. Lastly, there needs to be an appropriate IT environment and infrastructure to support agile development to facilitate frequent deliveries of quality software. In summary, these are the five recommendations for this phase: (1) establish a people-based change management strategy; (2) start with people willing to change; (3) involve and compromise power holders; (4) start with important pilot projects; (5) provides the necessary conditions for people to carry out their work.

(2) Implementation: Since there is a subculture willing and supported by senior management to work with agile methods, then the next step is to adopt them in practice in pilot projects. Following are the twelve recommendations identified as essential for the execution phase of agile methods in software

Table 3. Problems and challenges faced in the adoption of agile methods in POs

Perspective	Aspect	Sources
Organizational	Organizational culture and resistance to change	(LSR)
	Little or no stakeholder involvement	(LSR) (CaS01)
	The trend of mega information technology projects	(LSR)
	The problem with contracts	(LSR)
	Compliance with standards and regulations	(LSR) (CaS01)
	Support from top management	(LSR)
	The problem with delays	(LSR) (CaS01) (CaS02)
	The pessimism with information systems	(CaS01)
Technical	Lack of knowledge and experience with agile methods	(LSR) (CaS01) (CaS02) (CaS03) (CaS04)
	The ingrained use of prescriptive approaches	(LSR)

projects: (1) promote teamwork preferably with small and perennial teams; (2) involves, engages and satisfies customers and users; (3) ensure the quality of the code and the product; (4) establish the time of software deliveries preferably in shorter times; (5) train the team in the method and technologies used in the actual project; (5) provide tools to support the software development process; (6) monitor the progress of the project daily and visibly; (7) explore multiple forms of communication; (8) avoid allocating the same person to several concomitant projects; (10) meets the legal requirements of the organization; (11) establishes expectations of documentation; (12) experience emerging methods and practices.

(3) Learning: Within the scope of POs, the first adoptions of agile methods are lacking in theoretical studies. For this reason, the recommendations suggested in this phase were constructed based only on empirical studies. The last phase is about learning. It consists of two recommendations: (1) evaluate the adoption of agile methods and evaluate the product generated by providing feedback to power holders; (2) encourage the creation of groups or communities of practice.

5.2 Final Remarks

From the methodological point of view, the case study was the most appropriate option because it complemented the interests of the research and offered opportunities to see reality by understanding it and apprehending it in its integrality. It is worth emphasizing that the use of observation as an instrument of data collection was not possible because the observation would require an immersion in the environment where the events happen, which is difficult to accept by the selected POs.

The main motivation for the development of this study was the lack of structured information on the adoption of agile methods in POs and, at the same time, the opportunity to better understand the implications of adopting such methods in the context of the public sector, labeled as employing a Administration that is resistant to changes, with excessive formalism, with many redundant and unnecessary divisions, rules and procedures for its operation [15]. Many people are interested in innovative approaches to government – including the adoption of agile methods – but they do not know how to get started, so they need introductory studies.

The set of recommendations is intended to help POs introduce the vision of agility and modernity proposed by agile methods in order to increase the chances of succeeding with this approach by improving the quality of systems developed by the public sector. Not least, this research consolidates the results found in theory and practice in a results framework, thus forming a theoretical basis on the subject, making it clearer to researchers and professionals in the field that the agile software development applied in the framework of the POs has been supported by scientific studies.

Lastly, the results suggest that adopting agile methods in POs may be more challenging than in other organizations because people with little experience need to lead teams and projects to success by demonstrating positive short-term results, and in some situations they do not Have the organizational support and the environment necessary to carry out their work, depending on external experts. Although this situation may change over time, this research has found clues that in certain POs this process may be slower and more complex because it requires people to learn new behaviors and adopt new ways of interacting with others, being the problem Aggravated when the new work dynamics are in conflict with approaches rooted in the organization, making change difficult. In addition, some studies have shown that not all work environments have evolved with the same enthusiasm; The inherent culture of the organization may not correspond to the agile approach, causing failures in the design and process of adopting such methods. On the other hand, this study found indications that agile methods are feasible for POs. When successful, the adoption of agile methods has provided greater job satisfaction, where developers are more satisfied with the way in which they perform their work and customers are more content with the software product being built. In addition to that, the government is proving increasingly open and favorable to using such methods.

References

1. Dingsøyr, T., Nerur, S., Balijepally, V., Moe, N.B.: A decade of agile methodologies: towards explaining agile software development. J. Syst. Softw. **85**(6), 1213–1221 (2012). doi:10.1016/j.jss.2012.02.033
2. de Melo, C.O., Santos, V.A., Corbucci, H., Katayama, E., Goldman, A., Kon, F.: Métodos Ágeis no Brasil: Estado da Práticas em Times e Organizações, 9 p. Relatório Técnico, Departamento de Ciência da Computação, IME-USP (2012)
3. VersionOne VERSIONONE: 9th Annual State of Agile Development Survey. VersionOne, 14 p. (2014)
4. da Balbe, R.S.: Uso de tecnologias de informação e comunicação na gestão pública: exemplos no governo federal. Revista do Serviço Público **61**(2), 189–209 (2010)
5. COMPUTERWORLD Healthcare.gov website 'didn't have a chance in hell' (2013)
6. BR TCUa: Fiscalização de Orientação Centralizada (FOC). Governança de TI. Recomendações. Arquivamento, Tribunal de Contas da União, 71 p. (2014)
7. Goldfinch, S.: Pessimism, computer failure, and information systems development in the public sector. Publ. Admin. Rev. **67**(5), 917–929 (2007)
8. BR TCUb. Levantamento de Auditoria. Conhecimento acerca da utilização de métodos ágeis nas contratações para desenvolvimento de software pela Administração Pública Federal. Arquivamento. Tribunal de Contas da União, 42 p. (2014)
9. HM Treasury: Agile digital and IT projects: clarification of business case guidance
10. UK NAO. Governance for Agile delivery. National Audit Office, 35 p. (2012)
11. US GAO: Effective Practices and Federal Challenges in Applying Agile Methods, 34 p. United States Government Accountability Office
12. Iivari, J., Iivari, N.: Organizational culture and the deployment of agile methods: the competing values model view. Agile Software Development - Current Research and Future Directions, pp. 203–222. Springer, Heidelberg (2010)
13. Wernham, B.: Agile Project Management for Government, 371 p. Maitland and Strong, London (2012)
14. de Franco, C.A.C.: Análise da legislação para a terceirização do desenvolvimento de software na administração pública brasileira em relação as norte-americana e britânica, 141 p. Dissertação de Mestrado, Programa de Pós-Graduação em Informática, UFRJ (2014)
15. Saraiva, L.A.S.: Cultura organizacional em ambiente burocrático. Revista de Administração Contemporânea **6**(1), 187–207 (2002)
16. Vacari, I., Prikladnicki, R.: Adopting agile methods in the public sector: a systematic literature review. In: International Conference on Software Engineering And Knowledge Engineering, Proceedings, Pittsburgh, p. 27. Pittsburgh University (2015)
17. Yin, R.K.: Planejamento e Métodos, 4 ed., 248 p. Bookman, Porto Alegre
18. Bardin, L.: Análise de conteúdo, 279 p. Edições 70, São Paulo (2011)
19. Graham, A.: Como escrever e usar estudos de caso para ensino e aprendizagem no setor público, 212 p. ENAP Escola Nacional de Administração Pública (2010)

Using Agile Methods in Distributed Software Development Environments

Wellington Feitoza Gonçalves[1], Ivaldir de Farias Junior[2], Renata Kalina de Paulo Alves[1],
Pedro Luis Saraiva Barbosa[1], Herlon Ribeiro Parente Cortez[1],
Isaac Bezerra de Oliveira[1], Marcelo Mendonça Teixeira[3],
and Nelson Leitão Júnior[4(✉)]

[1] Leão Sampaio University Center (UNILEÃO), Juazeiro do Norte, CE, Brazil
{wellingtonfeitoza,Kalina,pedroluis,Herlon,
isaacbezerra}@leaosampaio.edu.br
[2] Softex Recife, Recife, PE, Brazil
ivaldirjr@gmail.com
[3] Rural Federal University of Pernambuco (UFRPE), Recife, PE, Brazil
marcelo.ufrpe.br@gmail.com
[4] CESAR.EDU, Recife, PE, Brazil
leitaojr@outlook.com

Abstract. Management is one of the factors with direct influence on the successful implementation of a project carried out in Distributed Software Development Environment (DSD), whereas mismanagement can result in schedule delays, loss of productivity and high costs. This article presents the benefits of using some of the key agile practices as well as the challenges encountered in DSD project management. The results were collected in quantitative research with the application of a survey among thirty-five professionals. These results indicate a positive contribution of the use of these practices.

Keywords: Distributed software development · Agile methods · Software engineering

1 Introduction

In search for competitive advantages, software development companies have undergone through a major evolution in their business, in which the development of software as a product has been accomplished by the distribution of their processes across cities, states and even in different countries, aiming to minimize costs, increase productivity and use geographically distributed resources; in this context, developing software in the same physical space, has become increasingly costly and less competitive [2].

Distributed Software Development (DSD) has provided several benefits to organizations that aim to develop projects with specific characteristics such as: productivity gains, low-cost skilled labor and the possibility of making use of some advantages over legislation [2]. However, as there are benefits in DSD, this type of work also presents several difficulties such as: physical distance, temporal separation, regional and

© Springer International Publishing AG 2017
T. Silva da Silva et al. (Eds.): WBMA 2016, CCIS 680, pp. 16–27, 2017.
DOI: 10.1007/978-3-319-55907-0_2

organizational cultures, languages, infrastructure and others [4]. Therefore, it is not interesting to handle this type of project as a traditional development project, and as stated by Oliveira and Lima [12], the adoption of agile methods/frameworks for the software development process can provide a better project management in DSD environments.

This article presents a set of agile practices to be used in DSD environments, aiming to minimize management problems in this context. Existing challenges and the critical success factors for the adoption of these practices in such environments are presented as well. This research intends to answer the following question: what are the main difficulties and benefits provided by the adoption of agile practices used in DSD projects? The article is organized as follows: Sect. 2 presents the usage of agile methods/framework in DSD environments; Sect. 3 discusses related work; Sect. 4 presents the research methodology; Sect. 5 discusses the results of the research; Sect. 6 presents a selection of agile practices most used in DSD environments; Sect. 7 presents the final remarks; and Sect. 8 presents the research limitations and future work.

2   Agile Methods or Frameworks in DSD Environments

The agile methods have some striking differences compared to traditional methods, and the agile methods or frameworks that stand out the most is the XP (eXtreme Programming), which states the use of some practices focused on development [1], and the Scrum framework, focused on project management [16]. Methods/frameworks have their principles supported in the Agile Manifesto, which is a set of values elaborated in 2001 by a group of relevant software professionals, among them Martin Fowler, Beck [3].

Agile methods or frameworks are people-oriented, defining that a process works well for those who use it, and stating that no process can have the ability of a team, therefore, the role of the process is to support the development team in their work [8]. In agile software development, the communication becomes faster and easier, in which team members share face-to-face ideas [11]. But even in distributed teams, the usage of agile methods/frameworks proved to be ten times more productive than traditional models, as stated by other authors [14].

DSD inherits all existing features from traditional software development, adding new challenges that are provided due to the specific context in which it operates, nevertheless, there are several motivations for adopting DSD, e.g., access to low-cost, yet specialized labor available in developing countries [4]. Some of these motivations have attracted more companies to use DSD. It becomes increasingly significant the number of companies that are carrying out their development process in DSD environments [10].

The use of agile methods/framework can be a positive approach when combined with DSD, that is, the use of agile principles in DSD environments can minimize the various challenges arising from this work model [7]. According to Paasivaara et al. [13], the use of agile principles helps to improve trust among the stakeholders of different cultures that are part of the process; in addition, the same authors reported that the usage of Scrum in a distributed development project enabled the increase of motivation of those involved, improved the communication, the software quality and increased the collaboration frequency.

3   Related Work

There are several researches that address the use of agile methods in DSD environments, and this paper will use as reference the studies described by: Audy and Prikladnicki [2]; Evaristo and Scudder [5]; Ryan and Sharp [15]; Shrivastava and Date [17].

As stated by Audy and Prikladnicki [2], distributed projects can follow a reference model. The authors consolidated the reference model (MuNDDos) to be applied in DSD environments, and their conclusions were based on their research, in which through some comparisons, it was possible to present the lessons learned that provided the identification of a category of factors (design, dispersion, stakeholder, organization and process of development) for the development of projects in DSD environments.

The studies from Evaristo and Scudder [5] focus at solving the challenges of DSD, however, the authors propose some factors that are important for the accomplishment of this work, such as: perceived distance, levels of dispersion, types of actors, development process and the existence of procedures and standards that can be used with the aid of agile practices in DSD environments.

As stated by Ryan and Sharp [15], agile distributed projects must follow some of the agile practices for success. The authors present in a research the relation on agility, team structure and virtual distribution to select the best agile practices. Their study was aimed to the generation of a set of best practices for the configuration of agile teams distributed globally. In this context, the authors' contribution was to select eight agile practices to be adopted in agile teams distributed globally.

Table 1. Comparison of related work

Approaches	Agile practices	Human factor	DSD support tool	Organizational factor
Audy and Prikladnicki (2008)	N	M	M	M
Evaristo and Scudder (2000)	N	PM	M	M
Ryan and Sharp (2011)	M	PM	N	M
Shrivastava and Date (2010)	M	PM	N	PM
This paper	M	PM	M	PM

M = Meets, **PM** = Partially Meets, **N** = No Answer.

The work from Shrivastava and Date [17] explores the intersection of two significant trends for software development, namely DSD and agility. The authors address the challenges faced by agile geographically distributed teams and proven practices for this type of development. The authors' research demonstrates some dimensions based on the literature, which are necessary for organizations to operate with agile practices in DSD environments. Table 1 presents a summary of the related works. The comparison criteria were chosen based on the main challenges of DSD.

The analyzed approaches bring significant results to the selection of agile practices in DSD projects. However, there are still gaps to be addressed, such as the criteria cited in Table 1. Thus, this work explores the use of agile practices in DSD environments and their importance in distributed projects by listing practices that improve the project management process in DSD.

In comparison to the other identified works, this paper focuses on the use of agile practices in distributed software projects and their benefits to the organization. This paper presents tools to support the DSD and a set of agile practices that can be used in distributed software projects to maximize results and improve performance during the execution of projects in DSD environment.

4   Methodology

This research used a quantitative approach, with the objective of collecting information from participants who work in the software engineering and participate in projects that use agile methods/framework in DSD environments.

The analysis and interpretation of the data identified the current performance of the use of agile methods/framework in distributed projects, the success factors for their adoption, the main agile practices in usage and the main encountered difficulties.

The plan for the execution of this research was composed by the proposed phases as follows: Phase 1 (study of the theoretical basis): during this phase, works from the main authors in the areas of software engineering, agile methods and DSD were researched and studied; Phase 2 *(survey):* in this phase, a questionnaire was developed and applied to professionals in software engineering; Phase 3 (analysis of collected data): in this phase, it was performed an analysis on the collected data. Challenges, difficulties, benefits and advantages related to the use of agile practices in DSD environments were identified at this stage; Phase 4 (agile practices in DSD): a set of agile practices used in DSD was identified.

The individuals that participated in the survey consisted of thirty-five software engineering professionals from Brazil and Canada, who work in companies that perform projects in DSD environments.

It was applied a *survey* of twenty-three questions for data retrieval. The structure of the questionnaire was based on the related works that served as basis for the accomplishment of this research. From the analysis of each work, some gaps were identified regarding the use of agile practices in DSD. Thus, the questions that formed the questionnaire emerged from the identification of these gaps in a way that could identify the dimensions that the agile practices could reach in DSD environments. After analyzing the collected data, a conversion was performed to a database, in which these data were studied using the IBM® SPSS® Statistics Base software tool, that enabled a descriptive analysis of the data and the generation of the tables and graphs in this article.

As stated by Wainer [19], the validity of an experiment is directly related to the level of trust that can be accomplished in the whole research process, that is, to obtain reliable elements from the theoretical basis adopted until the identified results, including the way that these are presented. Therefore, as a *survey* research in which participants respond to the questionnaire within their own environment, this research is subject to be influenced by behaviors that could not be controlled.

5   Results

This section presents the results from the analysis of the collected data on the usage of agile methods/framework in DSD environments. The consistency of the answers obtained through the utilization of the questionnaire revealed that this measuring instrument showed high reliability in the space where it was applied. The Cronbach's alpha value for this questionnaire was 0.843, considering the preference established by Streiner [18], which suggests that the coefficient values above 0.80 represents a high confidence level. Thus, by verifying the results statistics, it is possible to give a greater relevance and reliability to this research.

5.1   Identification of Participants

In order to identify the level of professional experience in distributed projects, each participant informed their years of experience with DSD and agile methods/framework in DSD projects. All the participants of the research have experience with DSD, as shown in Table 2.

Table 2.   Professionals with experience in DSD

Experience with DSD	Number of professionals	
	Frequency	Percentage
Up to 1 year	6	17.1%
From 1 to 3 years	10	**28.6%**
From 3 to 5 years	10	**28.6%**
From 4 to 7 years	4	11.4%
From 7 to 9 years	1	2.9%
More than 10 years	4	11.4%
Total	35	100,0%

Among the participants (Table 3), 88.6% already used agile practices in their distributed projects, 11.4% reported not using agile methods in DSD projects. Concerning the professionals who already use agile practices in DSD, 2.9% said that they have 7 to 9 years of experience, 11.4% have 4 to 7 years, 17.1% have 3 to 5 years, 31.4% said that they had 1 to 3 years and 25.7% said that they had up to 1 year of experience. No participant had agile experience for over 10 years, thus, 4 (11.4%) participants who reported having experience in DSD alone and had no experience with the use of agile practices in distributed projects were excluded from the results regarding the use of agile practices. The results related to agile practices are only valid to participants who have experience in agile projects in DSD environments.

Table 3. Professional's experience with agile practices in DSD

Experience with agile practices in DSD	Number of professionals	
	Frequency	Percentage
Up to 1 year	Referring to Fig.	25.7%
From 1 to 3 years	11	**31.4%**
From 3 to 5 years	6	17.1%
From 4 to 7 years	4	11.4%
From 7 to 9 years	1	2.9%
Not using agile methods in DSD	4	11.4%
Total	**35**	**100.0%**

5.2 Main Challenges in DSD Environments

To identify the main challenges in performing DSD projects, each participant contributed with information about the difficulties encountered in their projects, Fig. 1 shows that the *Communication* is the greatest challenge identified by participants, corresponding to 60.0%. And as stated by [6], communication stands out, as one of the activities of great importance among team members, also, Evaristo and Scudder [5] suggest the creation of communication patterns to minimize difficulties. And representing the lowest value are the *Processes and Tools*, with 11.4%.

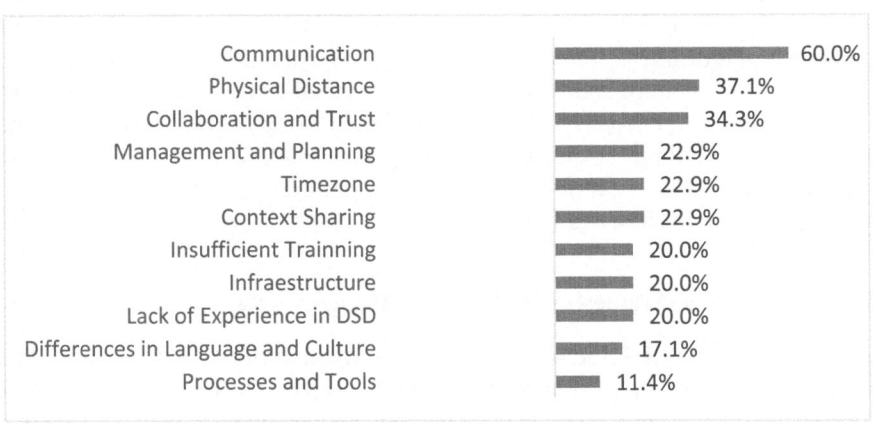

Fig. 1. Main challenges in DSD

5.3 Critical Factors for the Success of Adopting Agile Practices in DSD

To succeed in adopting agile practices in DSD environments, it is necessary to work on some critical factors in the team. The survey participants reported that *Motivated Teams* (with 71.4% of answers) and *Self-Managed Teams* (with 60.0%) are the main factors for success in distributed projects. Through the data analysis it was identified that the individuals with 1 to 3 years of experience with agile methods in DSD believe that the approach of a self managed team is the main critical factor for success. Professionals with less than 1 year of experience have the preference of keeping motivated teams as their main success factor. Among the professionals with experience from 5 to 7 years, the highest preference for the factor of success of a distributed project is to have an experienced coach and to keep the team motivated. And with 20.0% of the answers, *Specialized Teams* were considered as a factor without much criticality, as shown in Fig. 2.

Fig. 2. Critical factors for successful use of agile practices in DSD

5.4 Most Commonly Used Tools in DSD Environments

For a distributed project to succeed, it is necessary to manage all its parameters as well. Therefore, the use of tools has provided a better follow-up of the processes that are part of the distributed project and these tools have become critical to success in DSD. Respondents stated that the *Apache Subversion* (40.0%) is the most used software version control tool and the *Microsoft Excel* has 31.4% of participants' preference as a necessary tool for control and monitoring of distributed projects. Other tools such as *Redmine* and *Microsoft Project* had 20.0% preference among the participants as the main tool to manage their Projects. Other tools (CA-ChangePoint, Bitbucket, PivotalTracker, Smartsheet, GoogleDocs, Dropbox, Gmail and Skype) were cited and preferred by 40% of the participants, as shown in Fig. 3.

5.5 Agile Methods/Frameworks Used in DSD Environments

The "Total" column in Table 4 shows the overall value of participants who stated that they use agile methods/frameworks in DSD projects. Most of the respondents, (77.1%) stated they used the *Scrum framework* to manage their projects. Through the analysis of the collected data it was possible to realize that Scrum is the most used approach by professionals with 1 to 3 years of experience in the development of distributed projects.

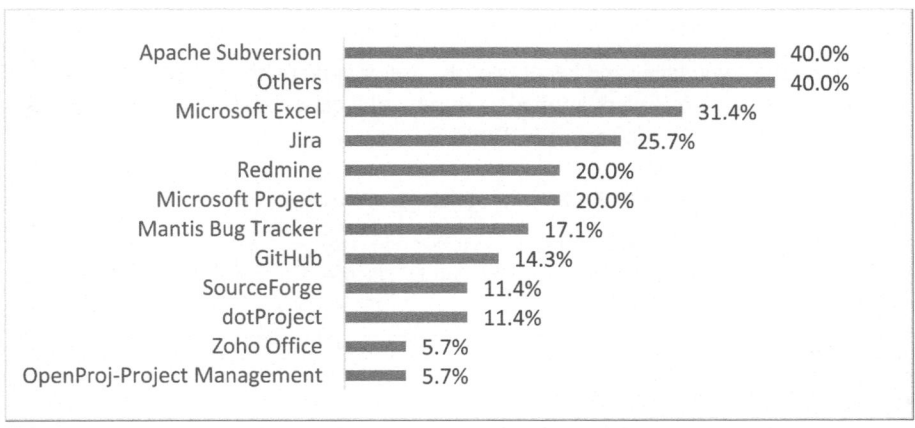

Fig. 3. Most commonly used tools in DSD environments

Table 4. Preference of frameworks in agile DSD

Framework and/or Agile method	Experience of the professionals in DSD projects, using agile practices					
	Up to 1 year	From 1 to 3 years	From 3 to 5 years	From 4 to 7 years	From 7 to 9 years	Total
Crystal	100.0%	0.0%	0.0%	0.0%	0.0%	**2.9%**
FDD	0.0%	0.0%	0.0%	100.0%	0.0%	**2.9%**
Kanban	12.5%	37.5%	25.0%	25.0%	0.0%	**22.9%**
Lean	25.0%	0.0%	25.0%	50.0%	0.0%	**11.4%**
Scrum	25.9%	37.0%	22.2%	14.8%	0.0%	**77.1%**
XP	16.7%	33.3%	16.7%	25.0%	8.3%	**34.3%**
Others	33.3%	0.0%	0.0%	33.3%	33.3%	**8.6%**

Even being the most used approach for project management among the respondents, Scrum is questioned by some authors about its efficiency in distributed teams, and according to Gregório et al. [9], has its main weaknesses in the lack of scalability for large and geographically dispersed teams. However, this view was empirically denied by Paasivaara et al. [13], who state that Scrum was used successfully in several large projects whose teams were distributed in several business plants. Other 34.3% of the respondents reported using XP, 22.9% using Kanbam, 11.4% using Lean, and the lowest values were found with *FDD* and *Crystal*, both with 2.9%. Finally, 8.6% reported using other methods. It is important to mention that 100.0% of participants who already use agile practices in DSD projects do not use only a single framework/methodology to follow their projects.

5.6   Benefits of Agile Practices in DSD

Concerning the advantages and benefits of the use of agile methods/framework in DSD projects, some questions were applied to retrieve the experience of the participants in this context. The results are shown in Table 5.

Table 5.   Benefits of agile practices in DSD

Benefits from the adoption of agile practices	Experience of professionals in DSD projects using agile practices					
	Up to 1 year	From 1 to 3 years	From 3 to 5 years	From 4 to 7 years	From 7 to 9 years	Total
Accelerate the Time to Market	23.1%	38.5%	15.4%	23.1%	0.0%	**37,1%**
Productivity increase	33.3%	27.8%	22.2%	11.1%	5.6%	**51.4%**
Better change control	6.7%	53.3%	33.3%	6.7%	0.0%	**42.9%**
Improvement in self esteem	27.3%	45.5%	18.2%	9.1%	0.0%	**31.4%**
Improvement in the system quality	25.0%	33.3%	33.3%	8.3%	0.0%	**34.3%**
Reduction of costs	40.0%	20.0%	20.0%	20.0%	0.0%	**14.3%**
Processess simplification	7.1%	50.0%	21.4%	14.3%	7.1%	**40.0%**

Respondents indicated that the *Productivity Increase* was the greatest benefit obtained from agile practices in DSD environments, with 51.4% of answers. As a result of the data analysis, it was possible to perceive that this benefit had its highest index among the participants who use Scrum, XP and Lean. The *Better change control* appears with 42.9%, followed by 40.0% who reported the *Processess simplification*. 37.1% reported that they obtained benefits in *Time to market,* 34.3% reported that their systems have obtained a better quality, and 31.4% identified *Improvements in self-esteem* of the involved professionals. The Reduction of Costs was the lowest benefit stated, with 14.3%, as shown in Table 5. In this scenario, 94.3% of the participants stated that the use of agile methods/framework adds positive values to DSD. Among the professionals with experience with agile methods in DSD, only two of them, with 1 to 3 years of experience with distributed projects, reported that the usage of agile methods/framework would not aggregate any value in DSD projects, and these respondents did not justify their responses. However, participants who stated that agile practices contribute to the development of distributed projects justified their responses, as stated by respondent A: "I consider it essential to use agile methods in DSD since they aim to streamline and organize activities avoiding damages derived from the distance of the stakeholders" and reaffirmed by respondent B: "There will always be improvements in the adoption of agile methods in any type of environment or project."

6   Selection of Agile Practices Used in DSD

After analyzing the answers from the survey, the main agile practices used in distributed projects were identified, as shown in Table 6.

Table 6. Identification of agile practices and respondents

Main agile practices in DSD	Experience of professionals in DSD projects using agile practices					Total
	Up to 1 year	From 1 to 3 years	From 3 to 5 years	From 4 to 7 years	From 7 to 9 years	
Collective coding	37.5%	37.5%	25.0%	0.0%	0.0%	**22.9%**
Clean coding	28,6%	0.0%	42.9%	14.3%	14.3%	**20.0%**
Requirements prioritization	27.3%	27.3%	27.3%	13.6%	4.5%	**62.9%**
Pair programming	25.0%	12.5%	25.0%	25.0%	12.5%	**23.5%**
Refactoring	30.0%	30.0%	30.0%	0.0%	10.0%	**28,6%**
Retrospective meeting	18.8%	25.0%	37.5%	18.8%	0.0%	**45.7%**
Daily meeting	24.0%	36.0%	24.0%	16.0%	0.0%	**71.4%**
Code revision	25.0%	33.3%	33.3%	8.3%	0.0%	**34.3%**
Others	0.0%	0.0%	100.0%	0.0%	0.0%	**2.9%**

It is expected that these best practices will help and minimize the possibility of errors in the realization of projects in DSD environments. It was verified that the professionals included in the research sample, denoted a more frequent use of three practices, as follows: *Daily Meetings*, with 71.4%; *Requirements Prioritization*, with 62.9%; *Retrospective Meeting*, with 45, 7%, as shown in Table 6. At the end of this research, it was possible to verify that the use of some agile practices in distributed teams proved to bring considerable benefits to the final quality of the product. Therefore, the main result of this research was the conception of a proposal of the main agile practices used in DSD environments.

7   Final Remarks

In this research, we analyzed the use of agile methods/frameworks in DSD environments and we investigated the use of the main agile practices, tools, challenges and critical factors for success in the adoption of agile practices in this area. This was demonstrated throughout the study and reinforced with the results of the research, in which 94.3% of participants stated that the usage of agile practices aggregates value to DSD projects. Thus, with 60% of the answers, *Communication* was identified as the main difficulty. Between the critical factors for the success of agile practices in DSD, the *Motivated Teams* factor stood out with 71.4% of the answers, and the greatest benefit elected by the participants, was the *Increase of Productivity*, with 51.0% of the answers. It was possible to conclude that this work contributed to the exploration of the existing gaps identified in Sect. 3 through the related works. And even by this work not being a definitive solution to the difficulties faced in DSD, it contributes to the management of distributed projects, providing a list of agile practices and tools most used for companies that are interested in adopting agile methodologies in DSD environments. The results showed that the use of the practices provides the optimization of project management activities. In this way, we conclude that the process of adoption of agile practices in DSD has contributed significantly to the development of distributed software projects.

8   Research Limitations and Future Work

One of the main limitations of the research is directly related to the number of people who answered the questionnaire, restricting the generalization of the results collected, however, it is important to note that the research results were sustained in the studied theoretical basis and the information extracted from the *survey* applied to the participants, in which each one of them collaborated with their professional experiences in the DSD area, which allows a good degree of security in the conclusions drawn.

As a suggestion for future work, a deepening in this area of study can be done applying experiments to validate the use of practices in distributed projects. Elaborate a research with more participants as well as the elaboration of a specific process model for the use of agile methodologies in DSD environments and their application in a real project to verify whether positive values are added during software development.

References

1. Ambler, S.: Agile adoption rate survey (2006). http://www.ambysoft.com/surveys/agileMarch2006.html
2. Audy, J., Prikladnicki, R.: Distributed Software Development: Software Development with Distributed Teams. Campus, Rio de Janeiro (2008)
3. Beck, K., et al.: Manifesto for agile software development (2001). http://agilemanifesto.org/iso/ptbr
4. Enami, L.N.M.: A project management model for a distributed software development environment. Dissertation (Master in Computer Science) - Department of Informatics. State University of Maringá (2006)
5. Evaristo, R., Scudder, R.: Geographically distributed project teams: a dimensional analysis. In: HICSS, Proceedings, Hawaii, USA, 15 p. (2000)
6. Farias, Jr. I.H., Duarte, L., de Oliveira, J.P.N., Dantas, A.R.N., Barbosa, J.F., de Moura, H.P.: Motivational factors for distributed software development teams. In: Proceedings of the Eighth IEEE International Conference on Global Software Engineering Workshop, Porto Alegre, Brazil (2012)
7. Fowler, M.: Using an agile software process with offshore development (2006). http://www.martinfowler.com/articles/agileOffshore.html
8. Fowler, M.: The New Methodology (2005). http://www.martinfowler.com/articles/newMethodology.html
9. Gregório, M., et al.: The seven sins in the application of software processes. UNIBRATEC - Brazilian Association of Institutes of Technology (2007). http://www.unibratec.com.br/revistacientifica/n2_artigos/n2_gregorio_mla.pdf

10. Herbsleb, J.D., et al.: An empirical study of global software development: distance and speed. In: International Conference on Software Engineering (ICSE), Proceedings, Toronto, pp. 81–90 (2001)
11. Niinimäki, T., Piri, A., Lassenius, C., Hynninen, P.: Studying communication in agile software development: a research framework and pilot study. ACM (2009). ISBN: 978-1-60558-694
12. Oliveira, E., Lima, R.: State of the art on the use of scrum in distributed software development environments. J. Syst. Comput. **1**(2), 106–119 (2011)
13. Paasivaara, M., Durasiewicz, S., Lassenius, C.: Distributed agile development: using scrum in a large project. In: Global Software Engineering, pp. 87–95 (2008)
14. Phalnikar, R., Deshpande, V.S, Joshi, S.D.: Applying agile principles for distributed software development. In: International Conference on Advanced Computer Control, pp. 535–539. IEEE (2009)
15. Ryan, S.D., Sharp, J.H.: Best practices for configuring globally distributed agile teams. J. Inf. Technol. Manage. **22**(4), 56 (2011)
16. Schwaber, K.: Agile Project Management with Scrum. Microsoft Press, Redmond (2004)
17. Shrivastava, S.V., Date, H.: Distributed agile software development: a review. J. Comput. Sci. Eng. **1**(1), 10–17 (2010)
18. Streiner, D.L.: Being inconsistent about consistency: when coefficient alpha does and does not matter. J. Pers. Assess. **80**(3), 217–222 (2003)
19. Wainer, J.: Quantitative and qualitative research methods for computer science. Update Comput. **1**, 221–262 (2007)

Gamification Use in Agile Project Management: An Experience Report

Igor M. Pereira[✉], Vicente J.P. Amorim, Marcos A. Cota,
and Geovana C. Gonçalves

Computer and Systems Department (DECSI), Federal University of Ouro Preto (UFOP),
Ouro Preto, Minas Gerais, Brazil
igormuzetti@gmail.com, vjpamorim@gmail.com,
ms_cota@yahoo.com.br, geovanacgoncalves@yahoo.com.br

Abstract. This study discusses the gamification in a software agile management process used by a computer laboratory. Laboratories like this have various details of organizations active in the industry. According to the events of the agile management process of the study, elements and mechanical games were used to improve the commitment and performance of collaborators and encourage follow-up of events in the process. Use of elements and mechanical gamification resulted in maintaining the commitment, increased by approximately 30% in the performance of collaborators and contributed to the improved tracking of agile management process.

Keywords: Gamification · Agile management · Software projects

1 Introduction

Given the need produced and deliver quality software products, organizations have invested in the improvement of their process [1]. Fogg study presents a model of human behavior change (Fogg Behavior Model - FBM) that can be applied in software development contexts [2]. FBM shows that people's behavior is influenced by three factors: motivation, ability and triggers. If a software development environment offer incentives to employees, they can become more motivated and thus improve their skills in the various tasks of their projects. Ensure employee motivation and engagement through gamification collaborates to improve software process [3]. According Pedreira *et al.* [4], gamification increases the involvement, motivation and performance of the employees in their tasks, through the incorporation of elements of games in the way conducting diverse activities of development and improvement software process.

Environments related to computer research laboratories such as other laboratories in others institutes of teaching and research, micro companies that have trainees, have different characteristics of medium and large companies. In these first environments mentioned, a most of the collaborators share time of their projects with other activities of their courses. Being formed by collaborators in the training phase, in the case the students, the leaders of these environments need to keep them motivated with their projects to control high turnover, build good teams, and ensure the quality of their

© Springer International Publishing AG 2017
T. Silva da Silva et al. (Eds.): WBMA 2016, CCIS 680, pp. 28–38, 2017.
DOI: 10.1007/978-3-319-55907-0_3

products [5]. Often in these environments, a drop in the productivity of students' teams is expected due to vacations and exams. Improving the process used in these environments needs to be a continuous search, to make it increasingly, easy and stimulating to be followed [6]. It is worth to mention that fledged companies are also concerned with the improvement of their process and may have characteristics similar to those of a laboratory and of new micro-companies.

Computing research laboratory used in this case study, named iMobilis, carries out innovation and research projects with teachers and undergraduates of the Computing Engineering and Information Systems courses of Federal University of Ouro Preto. iMobilis tailored the Scrum framework as its software process focused on project management. This study shows a tailoring of Scrum used in the iMobilis' projects and how the gamification elements were inserted in this process to encourage their follow. An analysis of the achieved is performed to verify how much gamification was effective. It is expected that this report can be used as a reference to other related environments that wish to replicate this study in agile process exactly as Magalhães et al. (2014) reinforces the need to disseminate case studies in experimental software engineering.

The remainder of this report is organized as proposed for case studies as suggested by Runeson and Martin [7]. Background is in Sect. 2. Section 3 the study case is described. In Sect. 4 the results obtained are presented and discussed. Finally, Sect. 5 presents the conclusions and Sect. 6 presents the directions for future works and the limitations of this study.

2   Background

Recent studies highlight the evaluation of the application of computing in the field of software development, in the education and in related areas [8, 9]. Good practices were demonstrated with good results, but in general there is much to be development with greater empirical validation, showing that there is still much to be explored with gamification in the area of software development.

Pedreira *et al.* [4] made a systematic review with the objective of mapping the use of gamification in the areas of software engineering. They selected 29 papers from digital libraries and annals conferences which were classified according to the area of the software process in which they focused and the elements of gamification used. Authors identified that the gamification's application in the area of software engineering is at an early stage. They concluded that the studies lack an experimental validation of the impact of their proposals according to the defined objective. Like most of the works shows a proposed of gamification, few validated its effectiveness in increasing the motivation and performance of the participants as often need to compare the results before and after the implementation of gamification. Studies' analysis showed that there is no standard methodology defined for the application of gamification. Most studies don't follow the initial stages of applying gamification, such as establishing the objectives, defining the characteristics of users and bases on this, define the elements that will be applied. Study showed that the elements most used are points, medals and voting systems. They further showed that the software implementation, tests and requirements management process are the ones that receive the most gamification proposals. There is still space for empirical validation in the process of rick management, project management and software validation. The events of agile project management are the focus of our study.

Cavalcante *et al.* [3] reports the experience of applying gamification in a technology solutions development company with the objective of improving adherence to organizational processes and of employees training. By well-selected metrics with evaluation of results by projects, teamwork was stimulated, increasing integration among employees, adherence to organizational processes by 40% and employee training by 214%. This work collaborates to show that the collaboration of the undergraduates through the gamification also happened and was beneficial.

Hamari *et al.* [10] analyzed several papers based on empirical methods that use gamification elements as a source of behavioral change. They analyzed 24 papers from academic databases and digital libraries. Most of the gamification elements used in these jobs is points, rankings and medals. Most of the works were in the area of education and learning and there were four papers referring to the application in organizations. According to most studies, gamification produces positive results in terms of increased motivation and engagement, as in performing tasks in a more pleasurable way. Three of the four studies on organizational systems have shown that gamification has a positive effect on those involved for only a short time. In general they concluded that the results of gamification depend on the context being analyzed and on the roles of those involved. Most studies lack control groups and are based only on users' opinions. That is, they describe the results statistically without taking into account the relationships between the users and effects on the context. Authors also realized that the characteristics and aptitudes of the participants influence the adaptation of each one to the environment.

Gamification has already been introduced in the academic area for the development of software artifacts. Dubois and Tamburrelli [11] proposed a methodology that can be applied at different stages of a software process. Thus, the gamification's work is divided into three sets of activities. First is the activity analysis which seeks to choose the best gamification techniques to be applied at different stages of software development. Second is the integration of activities that focuses on the development of modules to be applied in the software in question. Third is the evaluation of activities which consists in the use of the modules developed and the use of metrics to evaluate the advantages and disadvantages of the use of gamification compared to traditional techniques. Authors applied gamification techniques in student's projects constructing object oriented systems. As gamification elements, rules were created based on the analysis of the development code. Using Sonar software, a code analysis tool, was created analysis of the code according to standard metrics. To evaluate the proposed methodology, two development groups were created, and one group knew the metrics obtained by the other group. Competition between groups was stimulated. It was verified the improvement of some metrics in the group that had the results of the other group as a benchmark, providing an increase in the quality of the software development.

This study analyzed the agile management process of the iMobilis laboratory, designed a process of gamification for it, implemented and monitored for four months the results obtained empirically.

3   Methodology

This study was divided into three steps. In the first step the goal was to management analysis already used. This allowed an understanding of the process and aided in the identification of the gamification elements that could be applied. In the second step the gamification design was realized. In the third step, gamification was applied and data analysis was done to evaluate its impact.

3.1   Step 1

This step occurred during the period from October 2015 to March 2016, which corresponds to a university term. At the beginning of March 2016, a questionnaire was applied to the collaborators to know their vision about the way of working in the laboratory and the idea of gamification. Concept of gamification was discussed with all. At the moment the laboratory had twelve collaborators and eleven answered the questionnaire. To evaluate the effectiveness of this study, the questionnaire served to validate the students' willingness to participate in a gamified process.

Approximately 18% of laboratory collaborators said they did not feel recognized or rewarded enough for their effort in the laboratory. Considering that only 10% felt totally satisfied with this item, gamification could help increase the degree of undergraduate's satisfaction, making their work recognized by the team. Approximately 80% of iMobilis' collaborators said they expected to be more motivated by introducing gamification into project management. That is, the majority believed that gamification could motivate them more to carry out their activities of their respective projects. 54.5% of collaborators expected to have a greater commitment to their lab activities through gamification. With gamification, one hoped to increase the degree of motivation and consequently increase commitment, since those with the best performance would be recognized for their effort. Questionnaire also showed that all collaborators agreed to participate fully in the gamification process. According to the answers obtained the feeling of being recognized and rewarded for their effort was cited as the most expected benefit when deploying gamification.

In this study some software metrics were used for analysis and comparison effect of the laboratory collaborators' performance before and after the implantation of gamification. Spreadsheets and reports for analysis of metrics related to the term in progress were collected from October 2015 to March 2016. These artefacts were generated at the end of each week by Scrum Master. The metrics adopted are dedication, velocity and relative productivity. Relative dedication is the amount of hours worked over the amount of hours that should be worked over the weeks. Relative velocity is the number of points held on the number points that should be performed. Relative productivity is the relative velocity over relative dedication. In all terms, lab activities are divided into four sprints, with sprints one and three lasting five weeks and sprints two and four weeks. Each week, each collaborator must comply with at least 15 h per a week, which varies according to holidays and recess. Before implantation of gamification, the laboratory had an average relative dedication of 104.5% in the school period (15/2). It was a good performance on the part of the collaborators, since in all the sprints, the average dedication remained equal to or above 100% of the planned. Relative velocity has remained constant throughout the term, but at a reasonable level that can be improved. Mean relative velocity was 60% and the average relative productivity was 64%.

As a result of the analysis, iMobilis had a satisfactory level of dedication on the part of its collaborators. But it could improve, because with greater dedication on the part of the collaborators could improve the index of completeness of the tasks of the laboratory. In general, it was observed that iMobilis has a good working environment, with a friendly atmosphere among the members of the laboratory, which facilitates the learning and the development of the activities. And at the moment, it could be an environment conducive to the application of gamification.

3.2   Step 2

Second step was the development of the gamification project on the agile project management process used by iMobilis. This step occurred in the month of March and begins of April 2016. For describe the problem and the context, some students felt that their effort wasn't recognized enough at the end of the process. It was perceived that they hoped for a trigger that would cause them to devote more enthusiasm to the projects.

A laboratory collaborators' profile can be described. Students are young, with between 20 and 29 years. iMobilis has 12 collaborators, two female and ten male. They are focused at this moment on their undergraduate courses, committed to their activities, so that when they finish their graduation, they achieve a rapid professional ascent. They like immediate feedback love to get along with others, so they cherish cooperative work and learn by doing.

Laboratory is an environment of learning, research and software development, where to develop the proposed activities requires a lot of concentration and dedication on the part of the collaborators. In turn, it can become a very stressful and frustrating environment if the proposed goals are not achieved. Added to this is the accumulation of activities from the courses taken by the students, which can increase stress and decrease the level of commitment of the members of the laboratory.

For each collaborator it is defined at the beginning of the sprint which activities are desired according to their project. Work is individual, with goal of developing a research project, software or a monograph, for example. Collaborators are divided by teams according to project themes. Teams have the purpose of forming teams of work to discuss topics and to solve doubts. Teams aren't formed necessarily by the same number of people, but according to the projects development by collaborators.

To achieve the defined objective, each collaborator must carry a set of activities. That is, it is expected that each one will follow the planned schedule of activities together with the Product Owner, obey the rules of the laboratory and participate in the events and carry out the activities planned in the process of agile project management. It's on this set of actions that the implanted gamification system is based.

As a result of the gamification project, it was defined the adoption of a scoring system and a ranking as the main gamification elements to be implanted in the laboratory. As complementary elements introduced, but not less important, are the rewards, where we apply the state and the gifts as primordial elements in our gamifications process.

Rewards are critical to the ultimate goal of this study. As noted by the questionnaire, the feeling of being recognized for the work done to other members of the group they are part is satisfactory for the collaborators. State provided by being the sprint winner motivates people. Those who didn't win at first are encouraged to improve. And the freebies serve as an extra incentive to collaborators to seek the best possible score.

Scoring system was done as follows. A spreadsheet with the items that would be evaluated and the score for each was proposed for all. Then, at a general meeting, everyone involved helped finish up identifying and assigning the items and points. Thus, a consensus was reached. Description and scores for each item were recorded in a rewards policy.

Each collaborator earns points according to the activities performed each week and in the fulfillment of certain events of the process. Table 1 presents the events to be carried out weekly by each collaborator and his/her points.

Table 1. Events and scores

Events	Scores
Dedicate at least 100% per week	3
Dedicate at or above 75% and less than 100% week	1
Attend general meetings	1
Attend technical and validation meetings	1
Properly use the project management system	1
Build publishable tutorials on new technologies	3
Collaborate with another member offering assistance	3
Import the source code of your project into version control	3
Perform all planned project activities	2

Rewards policy establishes rewards for collaborators with the highest sprint score. Collaborators with the highest number of points per sprint are considered the winners. At the end of all sprints, we also had the winners for the whole school term, according to the accumulation of points obtained and a bigger reward was offered.

There is an item that provides the score to a collaborator who gives assistance to another. In this case this study treats two other elements of gamification, which are collaboration and competition. Taking questions with a lab partner through advice and tips is very common. It was supposed that one can't discourage contact with another. Gamification is an instrument of social interaction. The goal is to get as many points as possible, but that does not mean that you can't help another member in the lab. Believe that the exchange of ideas is beneficial to the development of activities and to those who help receive points for it, and whoever receives must report this fact so that it is recognized and validated by the other members of the laboratory.

Rewards policy has the mission to value and recognize the collaborators according to the activities carried out and their contributions to the welfare and development of the activities. Policy was disclosed to all and fixed on the wall of the laboratory as a way to enable consultation of all collaborators. Table 2 presents the rewards used.

Table 2. Gamification's rewards

Gamification's rewards
Recognition of sprint winners before the team at general meetings
Announcement of winners in the group of employees and employees of iMobilis on Facebook
Sprint winner team starts the next with 2 extra points
Winner of the sprint collaborator is exempt from paying the coffee box next sprint
Collaborator who adds more points during the four sprints will be totally exempt from his or her payment for the laboratory fellowship event

Under the rewards policy, the winner will be the collaborator who adds the most points during a sprint and there will be a winner at the end of all sprints of the school term. In case of draw the criterion chosen will be the relative productivity metric. That is, the collaborator who devote the closest to expected and more validate their proposed activities.

3.3   Step 3

Starting on 04/14/2016 the implementation of Scrum gamification in the iMobilis marks the beginning of the third stage of this study. It coincides with the beginning of the university's term (16/1). Scrum Master (student) is responsible for monitoring and evaluating the activities carried out. He/she is also responsible for overseeing all projects, collecting data and evaluating the progress of activities. In addition, he/she performs the dissemination of the score obtained from all members of the laboratory. A very important element in a gamified system is feedback, where everyone involved is aware of their performance at all times and what they can do to improve. With this, the notion of progression is felt as the collaborator carries out the activities.

Each week, the partial score with the score obtained by each collaborator is published through paintings on the wall of the laboratory for everyone to see. Thus, each member is aware of their performance and their current rank in the ranking. Result is also communicated via email sent to the lab group, along with the spreadsheet, reports and minutes of the meeting. At the end of the sprints the winners are announced at the weekly meeting before the entire team and it is fixed in a visible place, posters with the disclosure of the winners and the rewards received as recognition of the work done.

4   Results

This section presents the results of gamification at the end of the 16/1 school term, after gamification, and compares them with the results of the end of the 15/2 period prior to gamification.

4.1 Percentage of Non-conformities

Figure 1 illustrates the percentage of non-conformities observed in iMobilis after implantation final of gamification. For non-conformities, it is understood that events do not occur on the total of possible events per sprint.

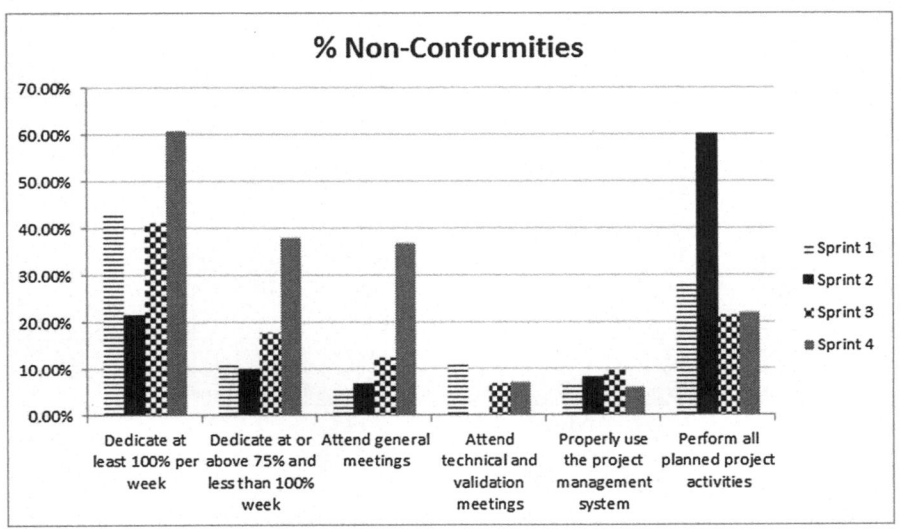

Fig. 1. Percentage of Non-conformities

In the X-axis we have the events that should be performed by all employees during the weeks of each sprint. In the Y-axis, we have the percentage of times that each event did not occur. Mean non-conformities in the four sprints were, respectively, 17.85%, 17.78%, 18.19% and 29.48%. These values were considered good. Intent of gamification continues to be to further improve these indices. It is worth noting that the average relative dedication of collaborators in the period 16/1 was 102.50%. That is, it continued to reach the expected after gamification. Before gamification (mean of the period 15/2), the relative velocity and productivity were 60% and 64%, respectively. After gamification (mean of the 16/1 period), these values were 82% and 79%, respectively. That is, an increase of approximately 30% in the average of these values.

As a result of analysis, concludes that gamification indirectly influenced the good level of productivity of the laboratory. Best scores are those that meet the estimated workload and are able to deliver their activities within the estimated timeframe. Thus, it ends up influencing the performance of all collaborators who end up wanting to win the proposed game. In a positive way, in the period 16/1 with gamification, the laboratory presented better numbers in terms of velocity and productivity than in the period 15/2 and kept the dedication above the expected 100%.

Table 3 presents the final individual results by sprints. We can see the winners in each sprint and a view of the performance of other collaborators. Names of all students were kept confidential.

Table 3. Individual final results per sprint

	Sprint 1		Sprint 2		Sprint 3		Sprint 4	
Position	Name	Score	Name	Score	Name	Score	Name	Score
1	R1	45	L12	37	S15	39	C6	31
2	B2	39	R1	37	C6	38	M5	30
3	A3	37	M4	35	M4	37	M11	26
4	M4	37	B2	34	M5	37	L13	25
5	M5	36	A3	32	B2	34	M4	24
6	C6	33	C6	31	A3	33	S15	21
7	L7	32	M11	31	L13	33	A3	23
8	A8	31	G9	28	L7	32	M14	21
9	G9	31	M14	28	L10	32	L7	20
10	L10	31	L7	27	R1	32	L10	20
11	M11	29	S15	27	G9	31	L12	19
12	L12	26	L13	26	L12	31	G9	18
13	L13	23	L10	26	M11	29	A16	15
14	M14	19	M5	25	A16	24	–	–
15	–	–	A16	24	M14	9	–	–

As Table 3 shows, there was a different winner for each sprint. This meant that the contributors worked hard to get a better score throughout the sprints, as a number of contributors alternated at the best positions in each sprint. We can also see a balance in the score obtained by all collaborators, with a smaller variance around the mean. Only in the first sprint there was a greater dispersion in the score between the winner and the last one. Two collaborators left the lab during the 16/1 school year, claiming to be very tight with other activities of their courses.

At the same time that a good degree of collaboration was observed among the laboratory members, there was also an increase in their competitiveness. In a general final meeting, approximately 70% of collaborators, the competitiveness between them increased after the application of gamification. However, no animosity was observed between lab members or a bad work climate. Or even some attitude is observed to the detriment of the item of offering assistance to another colleague of laboratory. This refers to the issue of winning the points in the race to be the winner of the sprint. Maybe most noticed that some colleagues were pushing hard to be the winner of the sprint.

5   Conclusion

Application of gamification to the agile project management process of iMobilis had positive aspects but also had negative points. As mentioned in the related works, the management of human resources in the midst of the application of gamification lacks valid experiences and needs a longer time for validation.

Initial idea led us to achieve some of the expected results with gamification as a maintenance of dedication and an increase in the speed and relative productivity of laboratory members due to the actual delivery of the tasks planned by the collaborators. The main reason detected for a motivation that can still be improved were the ancillary rewards to publicize and recognize the winners in each sprint for the work done. This is a symbolic reward that offers status to the winner. We have, for example, the options that involve financial costs like gifts or purchases of some materials or books for the laboratory or the students' project. It was proposed by the students also in the meetings, the distribution of scholarships for the participation in courses online.

As for the effect of gamification in the context of the motivation, we place it as a complementary factor for the complete accomplishment of activities by the collaborators, because the individual is also motivated with the knowledge acquired and with the experience obtained in the laboratory. One issue is being motivated with laboratory activities, another is gamification providing this motivation.

In general, the application of gamification to agile management of iMobilis was positive and relevant. Collaborators felt recognized for the effort expended in the laboratory, as explained above. Proposed methodology provided an efficient feedback on the performance of each one, an indispensable premise for the smooth running of the activities of any gamified system. Although the main method of evaluation is punctuation, which inspires competitiveness by nature, gamification in iMobilis is also notable for an increased level of collaboration among laboratory members.

6 Limitations and Future Works

Application of gamification in iMobilis is at an early stage and there are many ideas that can be applied in order to improve their processes. In addition, the construction of interactive software may provide the application of other elements of gamification in other software engineering processes not applied in this work.

In the gamification we report, individuals are passive in the process of evaluation. They perform their activities, earn points, But do not interact directly with a game.. For this, it is proposed the development of a software that allows the integration with the tools of support to the laboratory processes and immediately provides the scores as the user is performing and recording the activities in the events of the processes. In addition, this software could make it possible to consult online the score and activities performed by each collaborator, as well as providing immediate feedback to the scrum master.

References

1. Chaves, N.L.S, Santos, G., Cerdeiral, C., Cabral M.L., Cabral, R., Schots, M., Nunew, E., Rocha, A.R.: Lições Aprendidas em Implementações de Melhoria de Processos em Organizações com Diferentes Características. In: Workshop Anual do MPS - WAMPS (2011)
2. Fogg, B.J.: A behavior model for persuasive design. In: 4th International Conference on Persuasive Technology – Claremont. ACM (2009)
3. Cavalcante, N., Amancio, F.D.S., Nogueira, E., Jucá, M.V.R.: Uso de gamificação como auxílio para melhoria de processos: relato de experiência. Em: Simpósio Brasileiro de Qualidade de Software (2015)

4. Pedreira, O., García, F., Brisaboa, F., Piantinni, M.: Gamification in software engineering – a systematic mapping. Inf. Softw. Technol. **57**, 157–168 (2015)
5. Santos, R.E., da Silva, F.Q., de Magalhães, C.V.: Benefits and limitations of job rotation in software organizations: a systematic literature review. In: International Conference on Evaluation and Assessment in Software Engineering (EASE) (2016)
6. Da Silva, Q.B., França, A.C.: Towards understanding the underlying structure of motivational factors for software engineers to guide the definition of motivational programs. J. Syst. Softw. **85**(2), 216–226 (2012)
7. Runeson, P., Höst, M.: Guidelines for conducting and reporting case study research in software engineering. Empir. Softw. Eng. **14**(2), 131–164 (2009)
8. Ng, P.W.: Software process improvement and gaming using essence: an industrial experience. J. Ind. Intell. Inf. **2**(1), 45–50 (2014)
9. Stokes, Z.: Integration of gamification into the classroom and the reception by students. Theses, Dissertations and Capstones. Paper 856. Marshall Digital Scholar (2014)
10. Hamari, J., Koivisto, J., Sarsa, H.: Does gamification work? – a literature review of empirical studies on gamification. In: Proceedings of the 47th Hawaii International Conference on System Sciences (HICSS47) (2014)
11. Dubois, D.J., Tamburrelli, G.: Understanding gamification mechanisms for software development. In: ESEC/FSE 2013 Proceedings of the 2013 9th Joint Meeting on Foundations of Software Engineering. ACM, New York (2013)

Application of Scrum Maturity Model in SoftDesign Company

Raone Costa, Raphael Rodrigues[(✉)], and Alessandra Costa Smolenaars Dutra

Faculdade de Informática, Pontifícia Universidade Católica do RS (PUCRS),
Av. Ipiranga, Porto Alegre, RS 6681, Brazil
{raone.costa,raphael.silva.001}@acad.pucrs.br,
alessandra.dutra@pucrs.br

Abstract. This paper describes how the SoftDesign increased adherence of their agile development projects to Scrum. Several Agile Maturity models have been studied and, based on a Decision Making Model, the Scrum Maturity model was selected. Then, we could realize and implement the necessary improvements. The result of this work was positive for the company, but it generated a reflection between the compatibility of following a reference model and work with agility.

1 Introduction

Given the growing demand for agile development projects, agile methods are being adopted by many organizations in order to remain on the market [10].

Classified as Level E under MR-MPS [7], the SoftDesign was having difficulties to maintaining its adherence to the reference model since adopting Scrum, the process became more flexible, with a team which each member has autonomy to make decisions and a documentation less traditional is required. This current and open scope development proposal pleased its clients due to the focus on business value generation in less time.

Based on this, the main question, which brought the motivation to develop this work: How could we help the company during this transaction, from traditional to agile? How could the organization measure the efficiency of the new development processing?

The objective of this work was propose improvements in the SoftDesign software development processing. Then, the idea of evaluate the company under an agile maturity model assessment came up with the aim of measure and maximize the maturity of their agile processes and deploy and maintain in the organization culture, the Scrum agile practices.

Throughout the paper, just after a brief background, we will explain how the actual software development processing works. Based on that, we have our process improvement proposal, followed by the execution of the two improvements cycles, containing the evaluated projects, evaluation method, assessments, identified improvements and results. At the end, we will be sharing the feedback related to the work results, provided by the SoftDesign involved employees. We will also present the final considerations.

© Springer International Publishing AG 2017
T. Silva da Silva et al. (Eds.): WBMA 2016, CCIS 680, pp. 39–49, 2017.
DOI: 10.1007/978-3-319-55907-0_4

2 Background

2.1 Process Improvement

There is a consistent demand coming from the clients looking for less cost and a better software quality. Process improvements means understanding the existent processes and adjust them in order to increase product quality and reduce costs and development time [8]. According to Sommerville [8], two different types of approaches to software improvement and change are used:

- Process maturity approach: focus on process improvement and project management. The primary objectives of this approach are the product quality and process predictability.
- Agile approach: Focus on iterative development and reduction of overhead in the software processing. The key features of agile methods are the fast functionality delivery and responsiveness to changing customer requirements.

Regarding process improvement, we have the PDCA cycle. This cycle looks for, continuously, better methods to improve the processes. According to [2]: The PDCA cycle, or Deming's cycle, makes the processes involved in the execution of management clearer and more agile by dividing it into four main steps, which are: Plan, Do, Check e Act.

2.2 Maturity Models

Maturity models drives the companies to get software quality and productivity. Moreover, adopt strategies related to continuous improvement of their processes. In a classic approach, there are CMMI [6] from United States and MPS.BR [7] from Brazil, as the most representative ones [3].

With the significant growth of agile approaches in the software development, there has been a need for maturity models focused on agile methods. There are already several types of them published [5]. However, it seems that some agile gurus are not satisfied with their support. Consequently, there are around 40 different agile maturity models [9].

Adopting them, the agile community would be able to avoid anarchy and lack of organization during the project development. Among them, based on the group analysis, the most compatibles to this specific work are the Scrum Maturity Model [11] and Agile Maturity Model [1].

Scrum maturity model: According to Yin [11]: *"The Scrum Maturity Model (SMM) is a maturity model that aim is to evaluate organizations which use Scrum"*. The highlight is the strong relationship with the clients [11]. "The SMM model creation was inspired by CMMI area processes and, when possible, a mapping between them and Scrum practices was done [11].

Agile maturity model: According to the creators, Chetankumar & Ramachandran [1] *"The Agile Maturity Model was created in order to improve the agile software development, looking for boost the agile principles and objectives"*. Agile Maturity Model (AMM) is focused on the management of application development activities. It is based on CMMI and evaluated through five maturity levels. It has a regular relationship with clients and its focus is general software [1].

3   SoftDesign Development Process

The SoftDesign development process starts by a product vision. This vision describes the general product objectives, which are the users and about a future vision (roadmap). From product view, the Product Owner details, together with the users, business needs that may be handled by the software, generating a list of needs (Product Backlog). Before to start sprint 0 (zero), we have the pre-game meeting, where the project definition is presented to the team. At the end of the project, the team does retrospective meeting, in this ceremony, the team, PO and Scrum Master discuss about facts and artifacts, which can be used or avoided in future projects.

During the product development, Product Backlog changes constantly. Product evolution happens in sprints, usually taking two weeks. Before to start a sprint, the client and PO identify which backlog items are priority. The team identifies how many items they are able to deliver within the iteration window. This last process is called Sprint Planning.

After planning, the team starts construction and test phases for each selected item, ordered by the priority. Whenever sprint duration is over, the client reviews the results during a Review Meeting and provides feedback about the product for the next sprints. Based on the feedback received, the team does the retrospective meeting in order to perform adjusts to its work processing. Doing that, the next iteration tends to be better than the previous one. At the end of each sprint, the team deploys a product increment.

4   Study Approach

4.1   Maturity Model Choice

We have studied the main maturity models related to agile - Agile Maturity Model. Scrum Maturity Model, Agile Processing Maturity Model – its concepts and features allowing us make a more accurate decision about which maturity model use as reference.

Both of them contain five levels of evaluation, they are easy to apply and based on CMMI. Towards an analysis performed, supported by procedural model of making decision, the maturity model most adequate to apply was the Scrum Maturity Model, having as main point, to be exclusively focused on Scrum, which is the methodology used by SoftDesign (Fig. 1).

The SMM assessment method is composed of equivalent questionnaires to each maturity level. Applying the questions, we can diagnose the company adherence to the Scrum and to the model itself [11].

The SMM assessment method, according to Yin [11], has three steps:

1. Pre assessment: SMM structure of levels and their respective objectives are presented to the team. Furthermore, initial expectations about the assessment are discussed.

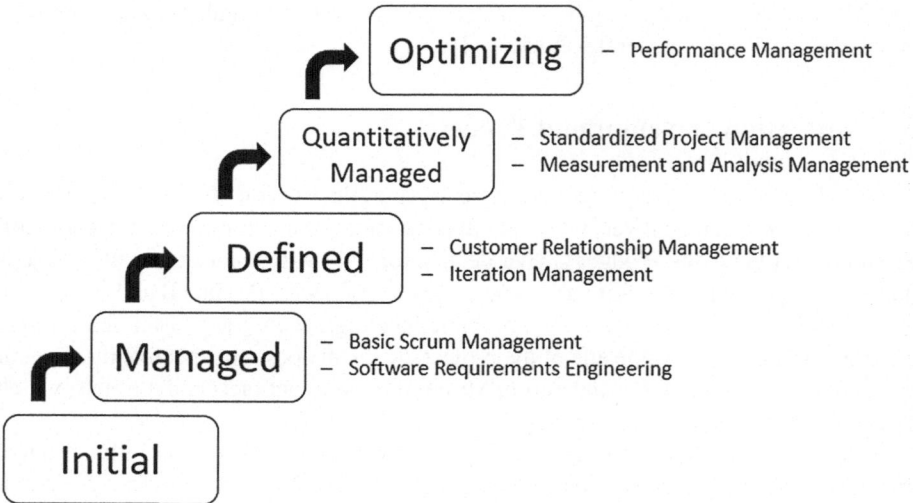

Fig. 1. Goals of each scrum maturity model levels

2. Assessment: In this step, the company, which works with Scrum, is designated to the Level 1 (Initial). After that, evaluation for Level 2 begins. If the result of the level 1 is positive, then evaluation for the next level is executed. The team has to answer the questions related to each maturity level according to its daily work routine of the project. It is important to say that all questions have to be answered positively in order to get the level applied.

3. Post assessment: It aims to extract the team feedback about the assessment processing and feel its satisfaction related to it. Furthermore, we can have a comparison between the initial expectations acquired in the pre assessment and the assessment result;

4.2 Initial Process Improvement Proposal

Looking for, continuously, improve the software development process adherence against the Scrum; this proposal was based on two PDCA cycles [4].

In the first cycle, each step consisted in the following actions points:

Plan: We have studied how to measure the actual development process adherence against the Scrum framework, how this decision would be made and which would be the evaluation scope. Do: Based on the planning created in the previous step, we applied a maturity model assessment on the selected projects. Check: The assessment results were analyzed and consolidated. Act: Based on the results analysis, improvements along the process were built and implemented, in order to get a better maturity level in the next evaluation. Nevertheless, one more PDCA cycle [4] will be required to make sure that the improvements were effective.

For the second cycle, each step consisted in the following actions points:

Plan: In this step, we planned when and how to validate the improvements implemented during the Act step of the first cycle. Do: Applied again the maturity model assessment, so then we can verify whether implemented improvements are being executed. Check: The second evaluation results were verified and analyzed. Act: It showed us that the company has evolved against the maturity level achieved in the first evaluation.

4.3 Evaluated Projects

In the first improvement cycle, we evaluated two projects. The first one, SAS –Audio Storage System. Its objective is developing a software to audio storage. Seven members including a Project Manager and Scrum Master composed the SAS's development team. SAS worked with Scala; Akka; JavaFX; MongoDB; JUnit; Git; Gerrit; Jira e Jenkins to its continuous delivery environment.

The second project evaluated was PEXH - Portal of Exams of the Hospital Alemão Oswaldo Cruz. To DevOps environment, PEXH worked with Java; Grails; Flyway; Hibernate 4; JUnit; JQuery; Asset Pipeline; Oracle DB; WebLogic 12c; Git; Gerrit; Jira; Jenkins; Selenium e Cucumber. Five members including a Project Manager and Scrum Master composed PEXH's development team.

In the second improvement cycle, we analyzed PDOC project in order to validate the implemented improvements. Android e iOS mobile project, which developed an application to facilitate the process called home medical consultation. The project worked with Java; MongoDB; Akka; JUnit; Git; Gerrit; Jira; Jenkins; Swift e AndroidSDK, emphasizing that, as well as the two first projects, the PDCO also works with Scrum and it is composed by the same team of the SAS project.

5 Proposed Improvement Process Execution – Cycle 1

5.1 Project SAS Assessment

Pre assessment: The specialist interviewed was professional A, who is Scrum Master of the SAS project. Based on an overview presented by us about SMM levels, she thinks that the company will be designated to Level 3. It is important to emphasize that Scrum allows adapting the model according to the team, looking for being objective instead of being precious.

Assessment: In the first Level 2 assessment item, we discussed Product Owner role and responsibilities, the company, instead of the client, nominates it. Continuing the assessment, the interviewed answered the remaining questions. As a result, SAS project was designated to Initial level of the Scrum maturity.

The project was compliance with 33 of the 36 Scrum practices related to the SMM Managed level. The following practices failed: Existence of Release Burndown artifact, Update Release Burndown according to the reported and Existence of Release Planning Meeting.

Post assessment: The results acquired during the assessment phase were presented. We discussed and clarified the gaps.

5.2   Project PEXH Assessment

Pre assessment: Initially, we have introduced the SMM model to PEXH's project manager, professional B. After the opening, we presented to her the objectives for each SMM level. Although aware that some practices could be improved, the manager chose second maturity level.

Assessment: The assessment for Managed level got started. The manager started to answer the questions and some doubts have arisen, but being clarified during the discussion. However, some questions to achieve level 2 have failed, what designated the PEXH project to the Initial level.

The project was compliance with 33 of the 36 Scrum practices related to the SMM Managed level. In order to be adherent to the second maturity level, the following Scrum practices were supposed to be active: Existence of Release Planning Meeting, Existence of Daily Scrum Meeting and Update Release Burndown according to the reported progress.

Post assessment: Having the assessment concluded and the level achieved, post assessment got started. The manager was not satisfied with the result but she understood that there are gaps, which need to be fixed in order to get a higher maturity level, especially related to Release Planning that caused two fails.

Another failure was caused by Daily Scrum meeting. PEXH project does not perform this ceremony. The manager said that she does not think necessary to perform it when few members compose the team and they work close. In contrast, the discussion allowed her to think about the benefits that Daily Scrum could bring to the project.

The failure in the Release Planning Meeting allowed her to remember the importance of having a deliverable date defined with a determined scope. This would facilitate on the features priority control and would increase the project progress visibility.

6   Identified Improvements

In order to get level 2, Managed, we identified some improvements and they needed to be implemented: Release Planning Meeting, Release Burndown creation and Daily Meeting execution.

We had a meeting with a project's Scrum Master to point out the improvements that needed to be implemented in the current process. The Scrum Master explained the procedures which the company works before to start a Project and also showed us practices used in previous projects which could have some link with the identified points.

6.1   Release Planning Meeting

During the improvements planning process was realized that organization does Conception and pre-design services with their clients. This service is executed along several days. During the meetings, the company looks for having the vision definition, the product understanding and minimum product viable prioritization.

In addition to this process and with the Scrum Master support, the company has been incorporating the Release Planning to the Conception service. This ceremony is intended to define the minimum product viable with clients contribution. The Release Planning was also included after pre-game meeting and before to start Sprint 0, having as objective to give opportunities to the whole team understands every product functionalities and solve possible discrepancies between the roadmap and team commitment.

In Fig. 2, we can see PDOC project's roadmap containing each release already planned with the client, followed by their respective deliverable date.

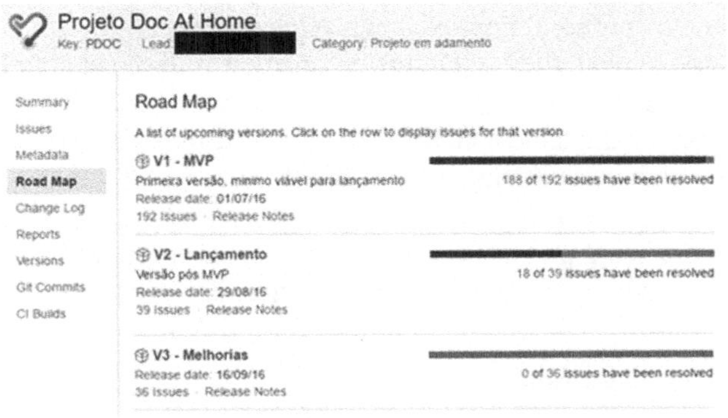

Fig. 2. Jira roadmap SoftDesign

Once this practice is implemented, the team can have a better visibility related to how much scope would need to deliver until determined deadline. The result of this practice also works as a tool to follow the releases development progress and, if the things are not going as expected, an agreement can be made in advance.

6.2 Release Burndown

Based on the work executed in the previous item, and using the minimum product viable proposal, the company, at the Conception moment, has the initial release deliverable date. As SoftDesign works with Jira to monitor their tasks and keep the projects on track, it is possible to use a functionality to generate Release Burndown chart.

6.3 Daily Meeting

During a conversation with the Scrum Master, we could see that in previous projects the meeting did not occur in the proper frequency due to a lack of culture under the meeting, since the Scrum Master did not remind the team about the ceremony and because of they did not have any news to say. However, without the meeting, the team identified that communication issues and impediments could be mitigated quickly.

Performing Daily meetings, the team has the opportunity to share knowledge about what they did in the previous day, identify impediments, create action planning to solve the issues and prioritize the work to be developed in the next day. Meanwhile, the Scrum Master is able to listen those impediments and give the proper drive to fix them as soon as possible, thus mitigating any impact in the sprint or release.

7 Proposed Improvement Process Execution – Cycle 2

In this second cycle, we were not able to evaluate the same two projects evaluated in the first cycle, because they were concluded. Therefore, the adherence validation against the improvements has occurred by a second Scrum Maturity assessment under PDOC project.

Based on this assessment result, we could verify the current maturity level again, and then measure the proposal improvements effectiveness.

By the first assessment, the SoftDesign company was designated to Initial maturity level. The group, together with the company, have been worked on developed those practices which are not implemented. In order to validate this effort, a second assessment would be necessary to measure the actions effectiveness.

This second Scrum Maturity assessment looks for validating if the implemented improvements were being part of the Scrum development processing, if they are being executed correctly and if now, they are part of project development culture.

7.1 Project PDOC Assessment

Pre-assessment: The professional interviewed was once again manager A. Scrum Master believes that in this second evaluation, the company would be able to not only achieve a higher level than the initial one, but also, reach Level 3 of maturity.

Assessment: After the pre-assessment, Level 2 (Managed) assessment begun. With the practices Release Planning Meeting, Release Burndown and Daily Scrum Meeting implemented in the company daily routine, Managed level was achieved successfully, in other words, every acceptance criteria for second level were completed properly. It shows that the company is able to manage the methodology, with all roles and responsibilities defined and following all framework meetings.

Once level Managed is completed, we applied the evaluation for Level 3, called Defined. At this point, the main discussion was the concept of tasks versus user stories, which ended up preventing the company from achieving maturity level 3, failing in 4 questions of 21, to the total.

During the Level 3 test evaluation, the lack of some practices were barriers to the approval. These are Break Product Backlog items into tasks within a sprint; Estimate sprint tasks; Update daily the estimates of running tasks and Estimate all items during Sprint Planning.

Post assessment: The improvements effort that the group performed with the company, since the results of the first model application until the second evaluation, led the company to reach Level 2 (Managed) of the Scrum Maturity Model. Unimplemented practices, that were impediments in the first assessment, were fixed and are now part of the current software development process and company culture.

Once the evaluation for the Managed level is completed, the test for the Defined level has started. The organization was disapproved in this last test, having as top offender, the concept of tasks. Scrum Master explained that the PDOC project does not work with tasks. The sprint work items are User Stories. Therefore, it is not the tasks that have estimates, but rather the stories that pass from phase to phase in the Kanban of the project.

The fourth and last fault obtained during the evaluation for Level 3 came from the fact that during Sprint planning there are items which have no estimate. Scrum Master gave examples such as research, investigations, design, cases known as spikes.

With the result of both assessments in hand, we could notice that the company maturity level has increased. Professional A did not show disappointment because of not being able to reach the Defined level of agile maturity, keeping in mind that it is necessary to evolve gradually. The initial step got started, the company is today, more adherent to Scrum, than previously, in fact, when the first evaluation of the model was carried out.

8   Work Result Feedback

An open questions interview was applied to the PDOC's Scrum Master, addressing the three improvement points, which were identified during the assessments.

Regarding the practice of Daily Meeting, the Scrum Master responded, *"Finding regularity in the dailies was very positive for the team. Often the team did not do the daily because they thought the information available on the board was enough and that there was nothing more relevant to be discussed. On the other hand, when doing the dailies even on regular days, we noticed that this helps us to communicate decisions that each person is making, identify risks before they even happen, and give that sense of agile that Scrum must have"*.

Regarding the implementation of Release Planning and Release Burndown, Scrum Master reported the following statement: *"The view of releases was treated in the first moment with the client, when during the work of 'Design and design' we looked for developing the whole vision. As soon as we could identify the MVP, the long-term vision was often overlooked, with the team focusing on the MVP. Keeping the release planning available within the tool and keeping this subject in constant discussion with our client was very important to support prioritization decisions. During the project, it is common for the Product Owner to lose awareness of the impact that the decisions made have on the releases, nevertheless, with the release plan and Release Burndown at hand we can help the Product Owner make better decisions and not lose the 'Big Picture' project."*

Project development team has provided a feedback as well. The team is composed by three Developers, a Quality Assurance, who is one author of this work, a Product Owner and a User Experience design. These feedbacks were collected through an open-ended survey.

Through the feedbacks, we realized that the development team did not have straight changes in their daily activities. However, they noticed the communication of the team has evolved adopting Daily Meeting in the PDOC project in comparison to the PEXH. Although the team is aware about this meeting in the previous project, as developer 3 mentioned in his feedback.

Among those interviewed people, there was consensus about the importance of the Release Planning ceremony. Now, the team can know more about the items that exist to be developed and their complexities, helping to maintain the correct pace and design the system according to future activities.

Therefore, while there were no significant changes in the routine of each interviewee, all developers mentioned the changes as benefiting the team as a whole, improving the way to people communicate, resolving impediments, mitigating risk, planning and managing their deliverables.

9 Final Considerations

Due to the transition from a traditional development approach to an agile approach using Scrum, SoftDesign felt the need to measure the effectiveness of the changes made and whether these were actually adherent to the new methodology implemented.

Taking into account a conversation between the group and one of the company managers, it was understood that the best option to solve the company problem would be the application of an agile maturity model, due to the importance of a process adherence assessment for them, once the organization has an MPS.br level E seal. The group investigated several models of agile maturity and, through studies, selected the one that best fit with the company profile, the Scrum Maturity Model.

With the model to measure the Scrum adherence, we applied the first evaluation. The company was not doing a good job related to the agile methodology, acquiring only the initial level of the model.

Despite the study carried out before choosing the model, not always a model is fully compatible with the reality of the organization. A maturity model is created based on a methodology and processes, and the way that a company works, is a reflection of its human resources, its clients and the market. Therefore, during the application of the evaluations, we had discussed several points regarding their relevance, which led the group to think: Is it valid to expressly follow a model of work and let it be evaluated by it?

Regardless of the divergences, the next step was the execution of another continuous improvement cycle so that, the practices, which were not being implemented, were implemented in the company, in fact. Once the improvements identified by the first evaluation of the model were defined and implemented, we executed the second evaluation in another project using Scrum, noting that, although it was a project different from the one initially evaluated, the team members were exactly the same.

The result of this second assessment showed that the company moved from an initial level in Scrum to the next level, managed, which means that the company has considerable management of the framework, with well-defined roles and artifacts. Furthermore, with all meetings taking place in the correct time, with a properly managed Product Backlog, among other practices, all while respecting the Scrum flow.

10 Research Limitations and Future Work

During this work, we had faced some difficulties and research limitations. One of them was to reconcile the development of this work with the company's work demand, since they had to participate in the meetings with managers and the development team in order to develop solutions and plan how the identified improvements could be coupled in the process and SoftDesign culture.

Another limitation arose when we applied the model evaluation for the second time, because between the planning time of the improvements and the second evaluation of the model, the initial projects were concluded and the company was adhering to other methodologies, Kanban, for instance. We could notice how fast the market demands a firm and how fast it needs to adjust to such requirements to stay active.

In conclusion, the growth of the company's maturity and its adherence to the Scrum was perceived by this work effort. However, the organization still needs to evolve as it was identified during the attempt to obtain Scrum Maturity Model level 3 (Defined), where the practices belonging to this level are not being performed by team members.

Future works can be performed to increase the maturity even more, executing additional continuous improvement cycles in order to support SoftDesign reaching levels higher than the Managed Scrum maturity, which level, the company is currently assigned. Preferably, focused on obtaining the higher and best level (5 - Optimizing) of the SMM, and ensure that, the practices implemented in the implemented improvements, are institutionalized within the organization.

References

1. Chetankumar, P., Ramachandran, M.: Agile Maturity Model (AMM): a software process improvement framework for agile software development practices (2009). http://ijse.org.eg/papers/agile-maturity-model-amm-a-software-process-improvement-framework-for-agile-software-development-practices
2. Daychouw, M.: 40 Ferramentas e Técnicas de Gerenciamento. Brasport, São Paulo (2007)
3. Pressman, R.S.: Engenharia de Software: uma abordagem profissional, 7th edn. AMGH, Porto Alegre (2011)
4. Quinquiolo, J.M.: Tese: "Avaliação da Eficácia de um Sistema de Gerenciamento para Melhorias Implantado na Área de Carroceria de uma Linha de Produção Automotiva". Universidade de Taubaté, Taubaté (2002)
5. Schweigert, T., Nevalainen, R., Vohwinkel, D., Korsaa, M., Biro, M.: Agile maturity model: oxymoron or the next level of understanding. In: Mas, A., Mesquida, A., Rout, T., O'Connor, R.V., Dorling, A. (eds.) SPICE 2012. CCIS, vol. 290, pp. 289–294. Springer, Heidelberg (2012). doi:10.1007/978-3-642-30439-2_34
6. SEI - CMMI for Development, Version 1.3 (2010). http://www.sei.cmu.edu/reports/10tr033.pdf
7. Softex.: MPS.BR – Guia Geral MPS de Software (2011). http://www.softex.br/wp-content/uploads/2013/07/MPS.BR_Guia_Geral_Software_2011-c-ISBN-1.pdf
8. Sommerville, I.: Software Engineering, 9th edn. Pearson Education – BR, São Paulo (2011)
9. Tomas, S., Detlef, V., Morten, K., Risto, N., Miklos, B.: Journal of Software: Evolution and Process 2013. Agile Maturity Model: Analysing Agile Maturity Characteristics from the SPICE Perspective (2013)
10. Version One: 10th-Annual-State-of-Agile-Development-Survey (2015). https://versionone.com/pdf/VersionOne-10th-Annual-State-of-Agile-Report.pdf
11. Yin, A.: Scrum Maturity Model. UTL, Lisboa (2011). https://fenix.tecnico.ulisboa.pt/downloadFile/395143154008/thesis.pdf

Modeling in Agile Software Development: A Systematic Literature Review

Fernando Mognon[(⊠)] and Paulo C. Stadzisz

Academic Department of Informatics, Federal University of Technology,
Curitiba, Paraná, Brazil
fmognon@alunos.utfpr.edu.br, stadzisz@utfpr.edu.br

Abstract. Agile methods have been used for over than a decade. However, there are limitations when using agile methods in complex, large-scale projects and in distributed teams. Traditional software design techniques, like modeling, could help overcome these limitations. This paper aims to identify modeling aspects in agile software development, presenting the state-of-art in this area, by means of a systematic literature review. The results show the use of modeling practices in agile methods, throughout the project, especially in the first sprints. The main modeling languages used are UML, informal diagrams, CRC cards and textual language. There are attempts of using agile with formal methods and model-driven development, without consistent results of the effectiveness of these proposals. Finally, we observed that the literature lacks conclusive experiments on modeling in projects using agile methods.

Keywords: Modeling · Agile software development · Systematic literature review

1 Introduction

Agile methods have been increasingly used in software development by companies of all sizes [1, 2]. One of the main motivations for the creation of the Agile Manifesto was to oppose the great focus given to processes in traditional approaches. However, this flexibility in processes does not preclude the use of instruments that can help build better solutions, such as modeling. Individuals and interactions should be valued more, but this does not exclude processes and tools as stated as one of the values quoted in the Agile Manifesto [3].

Modeling assists the process of design, allowing the materialization of abstract and conceptual ideas during the intellectual and creative activity of inventing or conceiving a solution to a system. The result of the modeling activity are models that, according to Ludewig [4], are artifacts that fulfill three criteria: mapping, reduction and utility. A model maps the original object or phenomenon, omitting details that do not interest in a given context for simplification (reduction) and have a pragmatic purpose (utility). Therefore, modeling has an important role to support the development rationale of the project, mainly in large and complex systems. Models can also help stakeholders communication, especially in distributed teams projects [5, 6].

© Springer International Publishing AG 2017
T. Silva da Silva et al. (Eds.): WBMA 2016, CCIS 680, pp. 50–59, 2017.
DOI: 10.1007/978-3-319-55907-0_5

Agile practitioners see modeling as having little value and utility when done prior to the beginning of software construction. Although, modeling with much anticipation can lead to mistaken decisions, when architecture evolves iteratively, decisions of greater difficulty of change must be taken in the first iterations [7]. There is also the perception that developers do not like modeling and documenting. Thus, if developers do not realize the importance of modeling, they will not use it [8].

After great interest from the software industry and some years of usage in practice, several empirical studies tried to identify the theories behind the agile methodology [2]. One of the main gaps observed in these studies about agile methods is the role of architecture on the software solutions [9]. Practitioners also call for more information on how to apply agile methods in distributed teams and large projects, in which the use of tools such as modeling can facilitate software creation and communication between team members [10].

The controversy regarding developers' motivation and the benefits of using modeling in agile software development, especially as the usage of agile advances to larger, more complex projects and distributed teams, justify to investigate the use of software design tools, like modeling. These techniques could help to improve the quality of solutions, facilitate systems maintenance and stakeholders communication, additionally to documenting the reasoning behind design decisions.

This papers aims to identify modeling aspects in agile software development, by means of a systematic literature review. In the following sections, we present some concepts about agile methods, the method used in this research, the results found, and the final considerations of this study.

2   Agile Methods

An agile software development is incremental, cooperative, uncomplicated, and adaptive. Incremental means that software functionalities are delivered periodically, usually in short cycles. Cooperative indicates that there is open communication among all those involved in the project, including customer (or its surrogates) and developers. Uncomplicated implies in an easy to learn and use process. Adaptive means responding to changes, even those coming late in the project [11].

There is a great variety of agile methods, but Scrum and Extreme Programming (XP) are those which presents more case studies in the literature [1, 2]. Recent studies also include Lean as one of the most used ones [12].

Scrum is a framework for software project management. It employs an iterative and incremental approach and it aims to understand customer needs and delivery value to them in short cycles, prioritizing most valuable features. Scrum is based on empirical process control, it means, decisions are taken based on what is known. It does not provide tools for software development, but is rather a framework to employ processes and techniques [13].

On the other hand, XP emphasizes programming techniques. It focus on communication and teamwork. Its main features are short development cycles, embracing changes, incremental software delivery, test automation, communication and collaboration [14].

In addition to the existent variety of agile methods, Scott Ambler [15] defined the concept of Agile Modeling as a practical approach for modeling and documenting in software development. According to this approach, models are used to understand what is being built and to help communicate. The main issue Agile Modeling addresses is how to create models in a more effective and agile way [15].

3   Review Method

This systematic literature review was conducted based on the guidelines proposed by Kitchenham and Charters [16]. The goal of a systematic literature review is to identify and analyze relevant papers on a particular question available in the literature.

The conduction of the review followed these stages: planning the review, search strategy definition and execution, paper selection and analysis. In the planning stage, the research questions were defined. The research questions that guided this review were:

- RQ1: What software design instruments do agile software development use?
- RQ2: How do agile software development industry and academy see modeling activity?
- RQ3: What are the modeling languages used in agile software development?
- RQ4: When is modeling in agile software development done?
- RQ5: Which modeling evaluation criteria are used in agile software development?
- RQ6: How is architecture defined and communicated in agile software development?

In the search strategy definition and execution stage, it was defined the databases to be searched and the search string. The search strategy included IEEE Xplore[1], ACM Digital Library[2], and ISI Web of Science[3] electronic databases. The following keywords were defined based on the addressed research questions. The **context** for this research was defined as related only to software. The interest was only for papers related to the agile software development, therefore the **population** is only for agile. The **intervention** in this paper is the modeling activity.

The logical combination of all elements from context, population and intervention provided the search string. The final string used for the searches was "Software AND Agile AND Modeling". The search was done including title, abstract and keywords. The search string returned a wide range of papers that were selected based on the inclusion and exclusion criteria.

Only original and not duplicated papers related to Software Engineering were considered. The paper quality and relation to the research in question were verified according to the following validation questions. All questions were affirmative for the paper to be included in the systematic review.

---

[1] http://ieeexplore.ieee.org.
[2] http://www.acm.org/dl.
[3] http://www.isinet.com/products/citation/wos.

- VQ1: Is the paper a scientific research (method is clearly described)?
- VQ2: Is the paper related to agile software development?
- VQ3: Is the paper related to modeling or design process?
- VQ4: Are the paper theme scope and limitations well defined?

The defined systematic review protocol was executed and the results are presented in the following section.

4 Results

In this section, the results from the search carried out in the databases are presented. Mendeley[4] tool was used to manage the files and references. The first search resulted 3939 papers. After first selection, based on title and abstract, and excluding duplicated papers 73 papers were selected. In the following selection step, based on the papers content, method and results 20 papers remained, related to modeling in agile software development. First author executed all selection steps and lately reviewed by both authors. Table 1 shows the amount of papers in each step for each database, and the search date.

Table 1. Search results

Database	Search date	Results	Title/Abstract selection	Method/Results selection
IEEE Xplore	07/26/2015	881	25	7
ACM Digital Library	07/29/2015	2.236	37	9
ISI Web of Science	07/30/2015	822	11	4
		3.939	73	20

After the papers had been read and selected, they were analyzed and classified according to the following categories: comparative studies and previous reviews about agile modeling, integration proposals between specific processes and agile modeling, practical aspects about modeling, architecture and requirements modeling in agile software development, formal methods and agile methods, MDD (Model-Driven Development). Table 2 presents the categories used to classify the papers and the respective references.

5 Discussion

This systematic literature review provides information from the chosen electronic databases answering the research questions that guided the review. In this section, the answers to the review questions are presented.

---

[4] https://www.mendeley.com.

Table 2. Papers selected and classification according to categories

Categories	Quantity	Papers
Comparative studies and previous reviews about Agile Modeling	2	[17, 18]
Integration proposals between specific processes and Agile Modeling	3	[19– 21]
Practical aspects about modeling	2	[6, 22]
Architecture and requirements modeling in agile software development	8	[23–30]
Formal methods and Agile methods	2	[31, 32]
Model-Driven Development	3	[33–35]

5.1 Software Design Instruments in Agile Software Development (RQ1)

Regarding design instruments used in agile software development, Stojanovic et al. [17] argues that the software architecture is based on object-orientated paradigm, domains, metaphors, and prototypes. The use of proofs of concept is encouraged when modeling is used, suggesting building prototypes that prove the proposed model operation. The use of components is considered in line with agile methods principles, since they accelerate the software construction, when existent components with well-defined interfaces are already available. The user interface definition, when applicable, assists in a fast feedback from users' expectation regarding the software usage and can be considered an instrument to help in the software definition [17].

Some papers presented tools to help the modeling activity. These tools are intended to making modeling tasks more practical. One example is the use of touch-screen boards in collaborative design meetings, that allows free hand diagram sketching [35]. Another tools (e.g., NORMATIC) aim helping to define the non-functional requirements. Although there is a lack of evidences of the effectiveness of these tools in real-world agile development projects [24].

There is also some proposal of formal methods use along with agile principles. They suggested that only safety-critical functionalities should be analyzed using these models. This approach demands the usage of proper modeling languages and tools assistance [31, 32].

Studies regarding MDD propose that, not only code could be automatically derived from models, but also test cases. However, this approach is criticized because it demands a high detailed modeling effort and the intensive use of tools. Debugging automatically generated code could increase the effort for developers, because it is not constructed on their own rationale [33, 34].

5.2 Modeling Usage in Agile Software Development (RQ2)

Modeling activity in agile software development is supported by the usage of sketches and diagrams. It helps understanding and designing the project. Requirements elicitation is also aided by modeling. The use of abstract elements facilitates communication between stakeholders that also include customers or their surrogates that could not understand software technical language [6, 22].

There are attempts to include modeling techniques to agile processes, since it is intrinsic to the development process. Wei et al. [20] suggest UML use along with Scrum. The proposed approach maps UML to Scrum practices. Requirements elicitation is accomplished by use cases and user stories. The software design, using UML in the sprints, should be in an iterative and incremental way, like Scrum. The proposed diagrams to be used are class, collaboration, activity, and state diagrams. Diagrams should be done collaboratively on whiteboards or flipcharts. The proposed model was considered of easy understanding keeping the process agility of Scrum [20].

The use of incremental modeling, focusing on the development of functional software, verified by tests, was evidenced in the studies. Tests definition using models is also reported in the literature [28, 29].

Due to more informal models creation process, in creative meetings, leading to informal artifacts, there is, if decided to communicate the diagrams to other stakeholders, the need for media transferring. This process may be done using tools to formalize the models in standard modeling languages, such as UML, but there are other possibilities like taking pictures of the created diagrams [6].

Abstraction concept is present in studies regarding modeling in agile software development. Due to participation of stakeholders that could not be familiar with technical notation, using a more abstract modeling level can enhance project understating. Depending on software construction demands, developers detail the necessary models. But, considering agile coding focus, the detailing is not encouraged, keeping the high level of models abstraction [22, 23, 28].

5.3 Modeling Languages in Agile Software Development (RQ3)

UML is the main modeling language reported in the found studies. There is also mention to informal diagrams, which may contain elements like boxes and arrows, or other pictures, such as databases, clouds or human representation. Although these informal diagrams do not have a formal specification, they may contain UML elements. Some papers mention the usage of Petri nets or Software Product Line. Studies regarding MDD always report the usage of UML, including customized UML profiles. Textual language is also used, for example in user stories. Additionally, papers mention the usage of CRC and robust charts. CRC are similar to UML class diagrams, and represent classes and their collaboration. Robust charts represent classes by their functionalities [6, 17, 20, 22, 26, 34–36].

5.4   When Modeling Is Done in Agile Software Development (RQ4)

According to studies found, modeling is done along all iterations. Each iteration consists of analysis, design, development and tests. However, there is more intensive modeling efforts in the first sprints. In these early stages, requirements are not yet fully understand and need modeling for their elicitation and better comprehension of the project. Architectural design is also more critical at this point, once decisions that are more permanent and difficult to change are usually taken at the beginning of the project. The development team, in collaborative meetings, creating mainly structural models, does the architectural definition [22, 23, 36, 37].

5.5   Evaluation Criteria Used in Agile Software Development Regarding Modeling Activity (RQ5)

There was not any research about qualitative or quantitative metrics, regarding benefits or limitations on using modeling in agile software development.

5.6   Definition and Communication of Software Architecture in Agile Software Development

Architecture definition meetings are usually collaborative, creating free sketches on whiteboards or paper. These artifacts, when already verified, by proof of concepts, for example, are digitalized, if this is considered an important information to be communicated with others. After a formalization of the diagrams, they are published in wikis or any physical visible place, such as walls. There are also proposals of coding tags to generate automatically the architecture documentation [6, 22, 25, 27].

Figure 1 depicts a synthesis of the use of modeling in agile software development according to the data collected from this systematic literature review. There is more modeling efforts in the initial cycles, but it is performed throughout the whole development process. The modeling activity is usually collaborative and supports requirements elicitation, better project understanding, and the communication among stakeholders. There is an attempt to use formal and MDD methods, as well as the use of components and feature modeling with agile methods. The main modeling languages used are UML, informal diagrams, CRC cards, and textual language. The studies presented a restricted use of tools for modeling and extensive use of whiteboard and paper sketches.

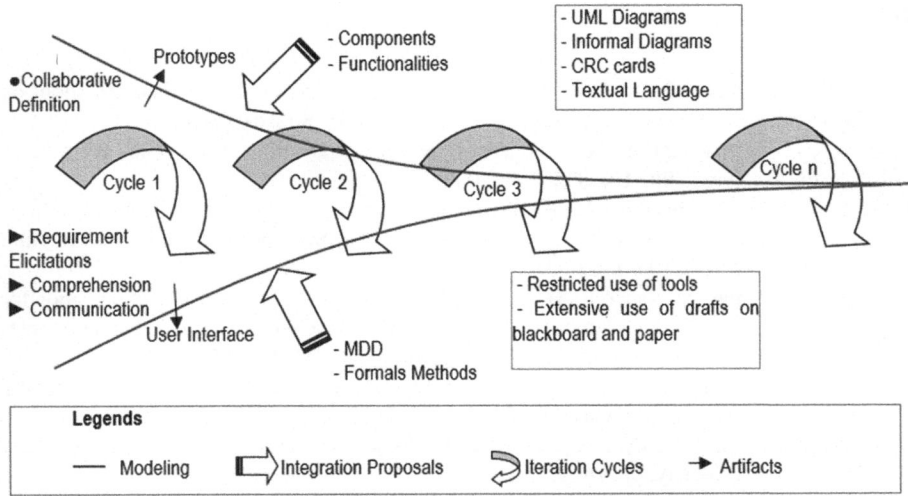

Fig. 1. Modeling in agile software development

6   Conclusion

In this paper, we verified evidences of the use of modeling in Agile Software Development. It employs mainly UML language, informal diagrams, CRC cards and textual language. There is an attempt to include formal methods and MDD in conjunction with the agile methods. Modeling is carried out throughout the development during each iteration, with a higher intensity during the first cycles.

The literature lacks, though, more experiments conducted in real environments. Most papers presents experiments making use of semi-structured interviews or questionnaires, which only present perceptions of those involved with the software development process and not the actual effects of using modeling in agile methods. In addition, many of the studies are proposals for different uses of modeling in conjunction with the principles of agile methods, among which only one case study is presented to validate the proposal, without a more extensive validation of the new model.

Regarding the limitations of this study, it is assessed that due to the choice of search bases and search phrases, relevant studies may have been omitted. The articles selection were performed by only two persons and can also lead to errors in the verification, since the analysis of the criteria are subjective, and could have different results if it was done by more persons.

As proposals for future work, it would be possible to study modeling languages that are more accessible and easy to understand, complete and have an adherence to the agile style, which involves an in-depth development. These proposals would be a counterpart to the use of UML, which, although widespread, is complex and presents many different diagrams.

We suggest also, that more studies could be done to establish evaluation criteria to identify the advantages and disadvantages of using modeling, so that it is possible to evaluate its usage impact.

References

1. Chuang, S.W., Luor, T., Lu, H.P.: Assessment of institutions, scholars, and contributions on agile software development 2001–2012. J. Syst. Softw. **93**, 84–101 (2014)
2. Dybå, T., Dingsøyr, T.: Empirical studies of agile software development: a systematic review. Inf. Softw. Technol. **50**(9-10), 833–859 (2008)
3. Beck, K., et al: Manifesto for Agile Software Development. http://www.agilemanifesto.org
4. Ludewig, J.: Models in software engineering - an introduction. Inform. Forsch. und Entwicklung **18**(3-4), 105–112 (2004)
5. Hadar, I., Sherman, S., Hadar, E., Harrison, J.J.: Less is more: architecture documentation for agile development. In: 2013 6th International Workshop on Cooperative and Human Aspects of Software Engineering, CHASE 2013 - Proceeding, pp. 121–124 (2013)
6. Cherubini, M., Venolia, G., Deline, R., Ko, A.J.: Let's go to the whiteboard: how and why software developers use drawings. In: CHI 2007 Proceeding, pp. 557–566 (2007)
7. Abrahamsson, P., Ali-Babar, M., Kruchten, P.: Agility and architecture: can they coexist? IEEE Computer Society, pp. 16–22 (2010)
8. Selic, B.: Agile documentation, anyone? IEEE Softw. **26**(6), 11–12 (2009)
9. Dingsøyr, T., Nerur, S., Balijepally, V., Moe, N.B.: A decade of agile methodologies: towards explaining agile software development. J. Syst. Softw. **85**(6), 1213–1221 (2012)
10. Freudenberg, S., Sharp, H.: The top 10 burning research questions from practitioners. IEEE Softw. **27**(5), 8–9 (2010)
11. Abrahamsson, P., Warsta, J., Siponen, M.T., Ronkainen, J.: New directions on agile methods: a comparative analysis. In: 25th International Conference Software Engineering 2003, Proceedings, vol. 6 (2003)
12. Kupiainen, E., Mäntylä, M. V., Itkonen, J.: Why are industrial agile teams using metrics and how do they use them? In: Proceeding 5th International Workshop on Emerging Trends in Software Metrics - WETSoM 2014, pp. 23–29 (2014)
13. Schwaber, K., Sutherland, J.: The scrum guide, p. 17 (2011). Scrum.org
14. Beck, K.: Extreme Programming Explained: Embrace Change, 2nd edn. Addison-Wesley, Boston (2004)
15. Ambler, S.: Agile Modeling: Effective Practices for eXtreme Programming and the Unified Process. Wiley, New York (2002)
16. Kitchenham, B., Charters, S.: Guidelines for performing Systematic Literature Reviews in Software Engineering. Keele University and University of Durham, EBSE Technical report (2007)
17. Stojanovic, Z., Dahanayake, A., Sol, H.: Modeling and architectural design in agile development methodologies. In: Proceedings of the 8th Workshop on Evaluating Modeling Methods for Systems Analysis and Design (EMMSAD 2003), pp. 180–189 (2003)
18. Erickson, J., Lyytinen, K., Siau, K.: Agile modeling, agile software development, and extreme programming: the state of research. J. Database Manag. **16**(4), 88–100 (2005)
19. ShuiYuan, H., LongZhen, D., Jun, X., JunCai, T., GuiXiang, C.: A research and practice of agile unified requirement modeling. In: 2009 International Symposium on InIntelligent Ubiquitous Computing and Education, IUCE 2009, pp. 180–184 (2009)
20. Wei, Q., Danwei, G., Yaohong, X., Jingtao, F., Cheng, H., Zhengang, J.: Research on software development process conjunction of Scrum and UML modeling. In: 2014 Fourth International Conference on Instrumentation and Measurement, Computer, Communication and Control, pp. 978–982 (2014)

21. Wang, F., Gan, S., Huang, L.: The research and application of the requirement modeling method on AM-RUP requirement process. In: Proceeding 3rd International Conference on Information Management, Innovation Management and Industrial Engineering ICIII 2010, vol. 2, pp. 643–646 (2010)
22. Baltes, S., Diehl, S.: Sketches and diagrams in practice categories and subject descriptors. In: Proceedings of the 22nd ACM SIGSOFT International Symposium on Foundations of Software Engineering, pp. 530–541 (2014)
23. Lin, J., Yu, H., Shen, Z., Miao, C.: Using goal net to model user stories in agile software development. In: 15th IEEE/ACIS International Conference on Software Engineering, Artificial Intelligence, Networking and Parallel/Distributed Computing (SNPD) (2014)
24. Farid, W.M., Mitropoulos, F.J.: NORMATIC: a visual tool for modeling non-functional requirements in agile processes. In: Conference Proceeding - IEEE SOUTHEASTCON, no. 978 (2012)
25. Durdik, Z.: Towards a process for architectural modelling in agile software development. In: Proceedings of the joint ACM SIGSOFT Conference – QoSA ACM SIGSOFT Symposium – ISARCS Quality of Software Architectures – QoSA Architecting Critical Systems – ISARCS – QoSA-ISARCS 2011, p. 183 (2011)
26. Hadar, E., Silberman, G.M.: Agile architecture methodology: long term strategy interleaved with short term tactics. In: Proceeding Conference ObjectOriented Programming Systems Languages and Applications OOPSLA, vol. 44(3), pp. 641–651 (2008)
27. Christensen, H. B., Hansen, K. M.: Towards architectural information in implementation: NIER track. In: 33rd International Conference on Software Engineering, pp. 928–931 (2011)
28. Pohjalainen, P.: Bottom-up modeling for a software product line: an experience report on agile modeling of governmental mobile networks. In: Proceeding - 15th International Software Product Line Conference SPLC 2011, pp. 323–332 (2011)
29. Hofman, P., Stenzel, T., Pohley, T., Kircher, M., Bermann, A.: Domain specific feature modeling for software product lines. In: Proceeding 16th International Software Product Line Conference - SPLC 2012, vol. 1, p. 229 (2012)
30. Paetsch, F., Eberlein, A., Maurer, F.: Requirements engineering and agile software development. In: WET ICE 2003, Proceedings Twelfth IEEE International Workshops Enabling Technologies: Infrastructure for Collaborative Enterprises 2003, pp. 308–313 (2003)
31. Black, S., Boca, P.P., Bowen, J.P., Gorman, J., Hinchey, M.: Formal versus agile: survival of the fittest. IEEE Comput. Soc. 42(9), 37–45 (2009)
32. Wolff, S.: Scrum goes formal: agile methods for safety-critical systems. In: 1st International Workshop on Formal Methods in Software Engineering Rigorous Agile Approaches, FormSERA 2012 - Proceeding, pp. 23–29 (2012)
33. Rumpe, B.: Agile modeling with the UML 1 portfolio of software engineering techniques. In: 9th International Workshop in Radical Innovations of Software and Systems Engineering in the Future, pp. 297–309 (2004)
34. Zhang, Y., Patel, S.: Agile model-driven development in practice. IEEE Softw. 28(2), 84–91 (2011)
35. Buchmann, T.: Towards tool support for agile modeling: sketching equals modeling. In: Proceedings of the 2012 Extreme Modeling Workshop, pp. 9–14 (2012)
36. Bruegge, B., Krusche, S., Wagner, M.: Teaching Tornado categories and subject descriptors. In: EduSymp12, pp. 5–12 (2012)
37. Durdik, Z.: An architecture-centric approach for goal-driven requirements elicitation. In: Proceeding 19th ACM SIGSOFT Symposium and the 13th European Conference on Foundations of Software Engineering, pp. 384–387 (2011)

Strategies for Reducing Technical Debt in Agile Teams

Marcelo M. Bomfim Jr.[1(✉)] and Viviane A. Santos[2]

[1] Institute of Technical Research of the State of São Paulo, São Paulo, Brazil
marcelomazini@outlook.com
[2] Federal University of Pará, Tucuruí, Brazil
vsantos@ufpa.br

Abstract. As the Technical Debt (TD) management is not yet explicitly part of the software development process, teams need to seek strategies to reduce TD, as well as continue adding value to the customer business. This paper presents a case study of how agile teams deal with TD in their daily work, observing which strategies and TD reduction practices are used. Data were collected through six interviews with Scrum Masters and technical leaders of four different companies. The results suggest that the teams are concerned with the software quality and seek to pay their TD proactively and preventively. However, several factors influence the decision on prioritizing the TD payment, such as lack of test coverage, team engagement, among others.

Keywords: Technical debt · Technical debt payment · Technical debt reduction · Technical debt management · Agile methods

1 Introduction

The Technical Debt (TD) metaphor is an analogy to financial debt. It means that by compromising the software quality to the detriment of some immediate benefit, it is likely taking on debt the long-term software health [1].

Seaman et al. [2] present some examples of the consequences of not paying TD, such as: high costs with software maintenance and evolution, software quality problems and decrease in the software lifecycle prematurely. Thus, it is important to pay TD gradually in a strategic way. As a result, the software project can be impacted positively, not only on increasing its maintainability, but also on improving team morale and motivation [3]. Linking TD to future risks can be one of the important actions to improve the TD management and visibility in order to minimize the impacts they may cause to the software. Still there is a need to identify strategies for reducing TD as a way to meet both software technical needs and business value [4].

Although the concept of technical debt has been used since 1992, there are still few effective strategies reported in the academic literature. The adoption of agile methods has provided satisfactory ways of dealing with the treatment of technical debts [5]. In order for teams to remain agile and add value to business frequently, it is always necessary to adapt the software to meet business changes at a sustainable pace [6]. Incurring in a technical debt may also generate customer value at some point, however to remain a sustainable software

© Springer International Publishing AG 2017
T. Silva da Silva et al. (Eds.): WBMA 2016, CCIS 680, pp. 60–71, 2017.
DOI: 10.1007/978-3-319-55907-0_6

development, the team has to manage TD and plan its payment [7]. Agile methods have practices and processes capable of managing and dealing with technical debts [8], such as refactoring, TDD (Test Driven Development), iterative management paradigm, pair programming, continuous integration, among others.

Most code debts can be paid with refactoring. Some authors, especially from the agile community, have suggested strategies for reducing technical debt, which complement each other [5, 7, 9–14]. In [13], the authors indicate that developers should balance available time in an iteration/release to provide value to customers and reduce TD. Other authors also suggest that the team use about 20% of the time from one iteration/release to concentrate efforts on reducing TD [5].

In this context, empirical studies on TD management are necessary to identify and validate the strategies and practices of TD reduction already proposed [1]. Thus, the objective of this research was to collect evidence of how agile teams deal with technical debts in their daily lives, seeking to observe and analyze which debt reduction strategies and practices are used. Therefore, the main research question is: "How do agile teams deal with technical debts in their daily lives?"

Thus, it was possible to verify whether the TD payment was managed reactively or proactively by the team. For example, if the debt is only paid if it is already impacting critical software elements or is paid when there is an opportunity for refactoring.

The secondary research objectives are as follows:

- Identify empirical evidence of debt repayment in software development teams using agile methods;
- Observe whether payment is made in a reactive or proactive manner by the team;
- Identify and analyze debt reduction strategies;
- Identify and analyze the influencing factors for paying TD.

This paper is structured as follows. Section 2 justifies and presents the research method, the selected cases and data collection and analysis. Next, Sect. 3 describes and analyzes the results, identifying how teams deal with daily technical debt, and which strategies and practices are used to pay off debts. Section 4 presents a discussion of the results with existing research in related areas. Section 5 concludes the paper presenting the research limitations and future work.

2 Research Method

The method used in this research was the case study. We decided to conduct face-to-face interviews, because it is one of the main methods used in qualitative researches to collect data. The studied cases were selected based on the intentional sampling method [15]. This approach is commonly used when the purpose of the research is to explore, understand or find evidence about the research subject.

2.1   Selected Cases

The research was carried out with six teams that work with maintenance and software development in four companies. The teams are identified with the letter of the company and a number, as for example: team A1, means team 1 of Company A. Table 1 presents some characteristics of the teams.

Table 1. Teams characteristics

Team	Project	Agile methods	Experience on agile practices adoption
A1	Maintenance of a fraud analysis tool for e-commerce	Scrum and Kanban	1 year and six months
B1	Maintenance of the basic product framework of the company that operates in the financial market	Kanban and XP	10 years
C1	Development of an incentive platform for shopkeepers in the resales of a large network of gas stations	Scrum	2 years
C2	Development of an incentive platform for shopkeepers who use a credit card machine from a payment network	Scrum and Kanban	2 years
C3	Maintenance of 40 projects aimed at incentive and award campaigns through an e-commerce to exchange points	Kanban	1 year
D1	Development and maintenance of public sector pension management software	Scrum	8 years

2.2   Data Collection and Analysis

Initially, a team daily monitoring was carried out to identify how they deal with the TD. We collected evidence of the use of practices and techniques to reduce TD. The initial observation was performed only with the A1 and B1 teams, as a pilot study. After that, a semi-structured interview script, divided into four parts, was developed and conducted with members of the selected cases.

Questions were asked about the experience of the interviewees and the projects of the teams. In addition, a list of debt situations was presented and asked if these situations occurred in the daily life of the team. Then, questions were asked to understand how teams deal with debts, looking to observe how debts are organized, discussed and paid. Finally, questions were asked to try to collect new cases of debt and situations in which teams had to establish strategies to pay them.

The interviews were conducted only with the Scrum Masters and/or technical leaders of each team, because they experienced the team's daily lives in technical matters as well as in process and business issues. All interviews were conducted individually and by face-to-face and lasted an average of one hour. The interviews with the A1, C1 and C2 team were only written notes. The interviews with the B1, C3 and D1 staff were recorded with previous authorization of the interviewees, and later transcribed. These last interviews were recorded with the objective of providing more fidelity and speed to the interview, since in the first interviews we only took notes. This process took a considerable interview time and was tiring for the interviewee.

The analysis of the annotated and transcribed information followed the strategy of describing the cases, using the explanatory construction technique, constructing an explanation of the case [15], and also making a comparison between them. Evidence was analyzed by subjects and was described qualitatively in the following section.

3   Results

Based on the data collected, this section describes and analyzes how the studied teams identify, discuss, organize and pay their TD. The strategies used by the teams are presented, making a comparison with the strategies found in the literature.

3.1   TD Identification, Discussion and Organization

Daily and weekly meetings, planning meetings, reviews and retrospectives were considered as a moment for discussing improvement points and dealing with software TD within the context of each team. The TD identification is performed manually by the teams during the contact with the code and artifacts of the software. Only the B1 team uses the SonarQube tool for code analysis and TD identification.

Four teams (A1, B1, C2 and D1) add TD tasks to the product backlog, even if it is implicitly (not highlighted as a TD). This strategy helped these teams manage their debts. The debts are controlled in the main backlog by the technical team. Thus, it is possible to prioritize them when planning or aligning the weekly tasks in the Kanban chart. It is worth mentioning some relevant statements of A1, B1 and D1 teams:

"The team registers a task in Team Foundation Server tool and estimates its effort. Thus, tasks enter the project backlog. In Sprint's prioritization, tasks were discussed and eventually prioritized. Most of the more technical tasks, the team itself attempted to absorb during the Sprints" (Team A1)

"(…) the team has the autonomy to refactor the problems encountered, but, for example, the refactoring task may take much longer than planned. I've always tried to make it clear to my team that if they find a bad code, they can fix it. If it takes time, we write down in a sticky note and prioritize for a developer to refactor it (…)" (Team B1)

"(…) the team began to register tasks in TRELLO tool categorized by technical debt. When the developer implements some task, he verifies if there is a debt to the related piece of code, because depending on the case, that task can be performed along with the business demand" (Team D1)

Other agile practices have also been identified, such as: refactoring (all teams), coding standard (A1, C1 and D1), code review (B1, C1 and D1), pair programming (B1 and D1), unit tests (B1), exploration of the definition of done (B1) and visual task board (B1). In this sense, it is worth mentioning the D1 team's Scrum Master statement, which states that the practice of peer review can help the team improve the quality of the code and also that the use of coding standards can contribute to preventing debts:

"The team itself realized that when doing the peer review, the code tends to improve automatically. I believe it is because the developer is more concerned about the code, because someone else will take a look, and he does not want to be ashamed of the other developers who are in the same room. It happens because at the time of the review the developers talk about the code… the quality of the code has improved a lot and the team has defined a checklist to review the code with a standard implementation guide" (Team D1)

3.2 TD Payment

Regarding debt payments, team A1 always tried to prioritize small refactoring left in the previous Sprint, because sometimes the team implemented palliative solutions to be able to deliver on time, and ended up leaving a mess in the code. It was common for the teams to perform refactoring as a way to improve code organization, for example: splitting methods to make them more reusable, using design patterns, and refactoring older code. However, if the refactoring affected other modules and incurred a risk to the customer, the team needed to share with the customer.

In the case of the B1 team, they also have the autonomy to prioritize refactoring in order to achieve continuous improvement in the software. B1 team also greatly explores the definition of done, and tasks are only finalized if the code is clean. Under pressure situations, palliative solutions can be employed, but after delivery, the team seeks to return to refactor. The team prioritizes debt if it is really disrupting development, otherwise it is not as necessary, as stated below:

"I'm just going to refactor something that is disrupting and something the most affects software development is software coupling (…) pure and simple software coupling is what most hinders and, in general, the refactoring efforts are mostly to decrease software coupling. Because software coupling generally destroys productivity, so you can't deliver what you need" (Team B1)

Time-consuming refactoring and refactorings that can cause software instability are shared with the product owner because the team needs to justify the hours spent and share the involved risks. In the case of C1 and C3 teams, they only prioritize refactoring if the software development time did not exceed the time planned for a business task. Only the most critical cases were approved by the business area.

In the case of the C2 team, some technical tasks were prioritized to be refactored, mainly performance related items, depending on the criticality. Tasks that presented risks to the customers or that did not generate value to them were difficult to prioritize. However, the C2 team includes TD tasks in larger tasks. The C2 team is uncomfortable with the implemented code, and on its own attempts to perform refactoring, even performing tasks overtime without charging the company. The D1 team prioritizes refactoring in two situations: when there are many bugs related to a specific part of the code or when the team has difficulty in understanding it. When planning activities for a Sprint, the team prioritizes refactoring tasks related to the business demands selected by the product owner.

Seven strategies are reported in the literature for TD payment, which are listed in Table 2. It is worth emphasizing the strategy of allocating a time during each iteration/release to solve TD. The strategies used by the teams studied were confronted with the strategies mentioned in the literature [5, 7, 9, 11–15], in order to find similarities and to validate their feasibility. The studied teams adopt four of the seven strategies presented in Table 2.

In relation to strategy I, B1 team reported that dealing with TD during the tasks occurs naturally in the team and there is no need to set aside additional hours to carry out possible negotiations. The other teams A1, C1, C2, C3 and D1 reported that they perform this strategy more explicitly, allocating a percentage of total Sprint time to make possible adjustments to the code. C2 team looks for performing small refactorings to improve performance, because it is a critical point of the software. The other teams use this time to perform refactorings to improve code organization and decrease coupling. This strategy seems to be much easier to implement in teams.

In relation to strategy II, only the C2 team often involves the customer or product owner, because all the tasks are in the product backlog and the team prioritizes the activities with the product owner every three times a week. Thus, refactoring items are presented and defended by the team and then enter the kanban board. Sometimes the team invites the customer to approve these tasks, but they face difficulty. A1, B1, C1, C3 and D1 teams often do not involve the customer or product owner, because it is difficult to convince the business staff that refactoring is critical to software sustainability, since it does not immediately add tangible value to the business, as reported by B1 team leader:

"It's very difficult to explain this to a non-technical person... but a software with technical debt takes you longer to develop than anything else. If I could explain to him that I'm not going to give you anything now, because I'll give you things later, because I'll have less technical debt... it's a very difficult conversation to have... it's much more feasible to mix business tasks with technical debts tasks" (B1 team)

In relation to strategy III, it was observed that B1, C2 and D1 teams also follow this strategy through the registration of technical debt tasks in the backlog. B1 team uses visual elements to evidence the technical debts of the project and its evolution, through TV panels in the development room, so that people can see the debts to be resolved. C2 team includes implicitly debts in the backlog, being only technical tasks. This strategy generates greater visibility of the items that need to be refactored. We observed that

Table 2. Strategies versus teams

Strategy		Teams
I.	Allocate a time during an iteration/release, trying to balance the effort between providing value to the customer and resolving the technical debts [5, 7, 13]	A1, C1, C2, C3 and D1
II.	Involve the customers and product owners by communicating them the value of paying off the project TD and asking them to consider it along with the new feature requests [10, 11]	C2
III.	Use daily team meetings, task boards, and burndown charts to increase communication and visibility of items considered important to the release, and also to discuss better solutions for reducing the risk of incurring in new debts [14]	B1, C2 and D1
IV.	Create a discussion group to meet periodically, review the performance of the system as a whole, and plan the changes for further reduction of technical debts [14]	B1
V.	Establish dedicated teams to pay off debts [5]	None
VI.	Organize special events called "ixit day" to identify and pay off debts [12]	None
VII.	Refactor a part of the system at a time. A complete refactoring of that part can give a broader visibility that the debt is being reduced, rather than refactoring into several small parts of the system at the same time [9]	None

these tasks can cause team discomfort. In consequence, the team members seek to pay the debts on their own in some cases.

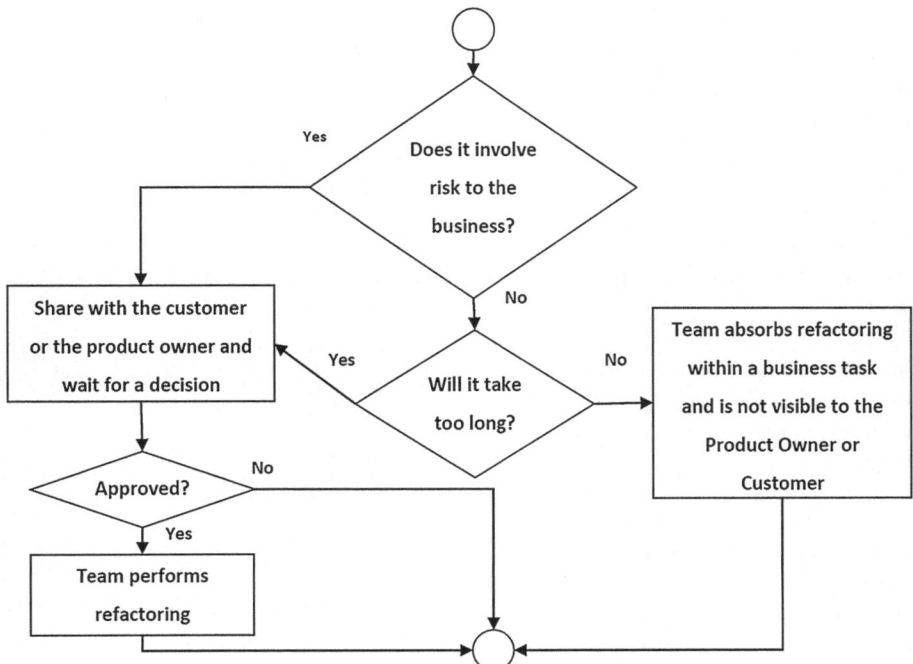

Fig. 1. TD payment decision flow.

Strategy IV may not be so common in agile teams, whereas A1, B1, C1, C2, and D1 teams have stated that they are in constant communication. Due to their work method, most adopt daily meetings, plannings, reviews and retrospectives. In addition, B1 team adopts this strategy in a organizational level by performing bimonthly meetings with the other teams of the company that use the framework to collect feedbacks, problems, and points of improvement. Then, they prioritize what needs to be worked on.

A new strategy has also been identified in the D1 team, which can meet both the software technical needs and add value to the business. According to the D1 team's Scrum Master report:

"Since we're handling this (specific) part of the code, we may improve it, and if we have a lot of trouble in this part, it's time to handle it" (D1 team)

The mentioned strategy recommends that a good time to perform a code refactoring is when the team is performing a business task in the piece of code with TD. In this case, a team member can add a few hours to the business task and at the same time perform the refactoring. This TD management strategy is proposed in [17] and states that debts should be mapped and estimated in the form of a list.

3.3 Influencing Factors

In addition to the TD strategies, a standard decision flow was observed to perform the refactorings within the teams, as shown in Fig. 1.

Table 3. Influencing factors versus teams

Factor	Responsible	General decision	Team
Concern of impacting some module because the team does not know all parts of the code to carry out a deeper impact analysis	Technical team	Not to pay	C1 and D1
Lack of test coverage or excessive manual testing	Technical team	Not to pay	A1, B1, C2 and D1
Members engagement by software quality	Technical team	To pay	A1, B1, C1, C2, C3 and D1
Company image degradation risk	Customer/product owner	To pay	A1, C2 and C3
Compliance with contractual clauses and/or end customer requirement	Customer/product owner	To pay	A1, C1, C2 and D1
Opportunity for software improvements	Customer/product owner	To pay	B1 and D1
Low impact for business and high effort	Customer/product owner	Not to pay	C1

When teams are facing the need to refactor a code, they evaluate whether refactoring could cause risk to the business or whether the customer is already at risk, justifying the need for refactoring. If there is risk, the customer or product owner product are triggered. Thus, the customer or product owner decide whether to approve the TD payment. If they do not approve it, the debt can be forgotten or delayed. If there is no direct risk to the customer and the team is sure that it will not affect other software modules, the team checks the effort required for the refactoring. If the effort required is relatively small, the team tries to absorb the refactoring within some related business task. If the effort is large and the team is unable to absorb the refactoring, the customer or product owner is triggered for decision making.

When the decision to pay off TD is passed on to the customer or product owner, the factors that influence it are different because it has been observed that they need to be related to something critical to the business or to part of their strategy. Table 3 shows the influencing factors observed in the teams divided by those responsible for the decision to pay the debt: technical team or customer/product owner. Factors were identified based on the evidence collected from interview answers.

4   Discussion

Based on only the cases studied, the treatment of technical debts is a natural practice in the daily activities of the studied agile teams, even implicitly in their work process. Teams need to maintain the software technical excellence in order to sustain and increase team agility [18]. In this sense, the result of this study shows that the studied teams value the code quality of their applications and prioritize refactorings related to the source code frequently and autonomously as much as possible. Quality attributes such as maintainability and performance are also constantly observed by teams as the aspect of refactoring.

Four of the teams (A1, B1, C2 and D1) record debt payment tasks on the project's main backlog and estimate the time taken to complete the negotiation, even if implicitly (not highlighted as a technical debt). These tasks are not necessarily visible to the product owner and the customer, because there are some concerns about involving the customer or the product owner to discuss code quality problems. However, they are controlled in the main backlog by the technical team, and such practice allows for further prioritization when planning or aligning weekly tasks. This result reinforces the TD management models proposed by [16, 17]. The models can be incorporated into teams in a more natural way, since they get already used to register technical issues in the backlog, being possible to categorize them through colors, as recommended by [16]. For teams using Kanban, the use of colors according to the categories of the backlog items can promote greater visibility to these items, and may even generate a psychological effect in the team. This may help the team to remember existing debts, as Shriver [14] suggests.

The TD payment is treated with some caution by the teams, as it may involve risks to the software operation. Paying a debt can impact something that is working, for example. When teams are facing a code that needs to be refactored, the team checks to see if the refactoring can negatively affect the customer and if there is a risk to the business. Small refactoring is prioritized by the team itself, due to members engagement on software quality, absorbing refactoring tasks within iterations. In cases where teams can not absorb debt payment, the customer or product owner is consulted for prioritization, when it involves something more critical or disturbs the team. Thus, risk management is necessary as part of the decision-making process for TD payment, and techniques can be incorporated to assist the teams. As mentioned by [19], TD can have negative effects in the form of poorly managed risks.

The weekly meetings, plannings, daily meetings, reviews and retrospectives, are considered as a moment of discussion about improvement and TD treatment. This result contributes with empirical data to the study presented by [8], which verified that the practices of the agile methods promote a greater technical debt perception, mainly the iterative process, reviews and retrospectives.

In one of the teams (B1) it was identified that it explores the definition of done to determine if the task was completed. This reduces the risk of incurring in new debts. Along with a coding standard and code review, these practices can help increase code quality. Peer review can have a psychological effect on the team, forcing its members to perform a more organized and readable coding. This reaffirms that agile methods have components capable of dealing with TD [8].

While all teams involve customers or product owners in more critical cases that involve serious risks, only one team actually engages them on a frequent basis. There is some concern among teams about involving the customer or product owner to discuss code quality issues, making it more difficult to support refactoring. In some cases, TD issues may expose a team technical weakness.

Overall, it is difficult to convince the business that refactoring is critical to software sustainability because it does not immediately add tangible value to the business. This argument reinforces the idea presented by [4], which mentions that it is necessary to seek TD reduction strategies that meet both software technical needs and business value.

5 Conclusions and Future Work

The cases presented in this paper present evidence from the technical leaders' and Scrum Masters' perspective of how six agile teams from the Brazilian software industry deal with TD in a daily basis. The teams studied seek to pay TD proactively and preventively, when a payment opportunity is found, preferably in the following iterations that the debt was identify. However, obstacles are found and many factors influence the decision to prioritize TD, such as: lack of tests coverage, compliance with contractual clauses, and risk of company image degradation, among others. We have noticed that the risk of impacting an existing complex code, may inhibit its refactoring.

The teams denote some autonomy to prioritize small refactorings and do them following some strategies discussed in this study. This autonomy is related to agile principles, which guide teams to maintain and value the software technical excellence, in order to sustain and increase team agility. The big challenge is still to pay TD and at the same time generate value to the business, mainly to be able to approve the payment by the stakeholders.

Even presenting limitations, such as: limited access to project documents at the initial observation phase and research results evidenced basically by the interview responses, this study can contribute to the TD management area. Software development teams can benefit from organizing a plan to reduce their technical debts, and incorporating activities in their software development process, according to their context.

As a proposal for future studies, it would be interesting to carry out a research with non-technical stakeholders, investigating how the technical teams approach TD issues with customers and product owners, verifying the risks that are assumed when deciding not to pay them. This study could also be conducted with other types of data collection sources, such as observations, documents analysis, and tool data analysis. Quantitative information could be drawn from agile team projects, for example, average time spent on projects to reduce TD. It is also possible to perform the same work with a larger number of teams and to use the Grounded Theory method to seek for a theory involving the TD management in the agile teams context.

Acknowledgment. The authors thank all the companies and professionals who participated in this research.

References

1. Li, Z., Avgeriou, P., Liang, P.: A systematic mapping study on technical debt and its management. J. Syst. Softw. **101**, 193–220 (2015)
2. Seaman, C., Guo, Y., Izurieta, C., Cai, Y., Zazworka, N., Shull, F., Vetrò, A.: Using technical debt data in decision making: potential decision approaches. In: Proceeding of the 3rd International Workshop on Managing Technical Debt, pp. 45–48. IEEE (2012)
3. Spínola, R.O., Zazworka, N., Vetrò, A., Seaman, C., Shull, F.: Investigating technical debt folklore: shedding some light on technical debt opinion. In: Proceedings of the 4th International Workshop on Managing Technical Debt, pp. 1–7. IEEE (2013)
4. Kruchten, P., Nord, R.L., Ozkaya, I., Falessi, D.: Technical debt: towards a crisper definition report on the 4th international workshop on managing technical debt. ACM SIGSOFT Softw. Eng. Notes **38**(5), 51–54 (2013)
5. Codabux, Z. Williams, B.: Managing technical debt: an industrial case study. In: Proceedings of the 4th International Workshop on Managing Technical Debt, pp. 8–15. IEEE (2013)
6. Bavani, R.: Distributed agile, agile testing, and technical debt. IEEE Softw. **29**(6), 28–33 (2012)
7. Lim, E., Taksande, N., Seaman, C.: A balancing act: what software practitioners have to say about technical debt. Softw. IEEE **29**(6), 22–27 (2012)
8. Holvitie, J., Leppanen, V., Hyrynsalmi, S.: Technical debt and the effect of agile software development practices on it-an industry practitioner survey. In: Proceedings of the 6th International Workshop on Managing Technical Debt, pp. 35–42. IEEE (2014)
9. Krishna, V., Basu, A.: Minimizing technical debt: developer's viewpoint. In: Proceedings of the ICSEMA 2012, Chennai (2012)
10. Kruchten, P.: Strategic management of technical debt: tutorial synopsis. In: Proceedings of the 12th International Conference on Quality Software (2012)
11. Laribbe, D.: Using agile techniques to pay back technical debt. MSDN Mag. (2009). http://msdn.microsoft.com/en-us/magazine/ee819135.aspx
12. Morgenthaler, J.D., Gridnev, M., Sauciuc, R., Bhansali, S.: Searching for build debt: experiences managing technical debt at Google. In: Proceedings of the Third International Workshop on Managing Technical Debt, pp. 1–6. IEEE (2012)
13. Power, K.: Understanding the impact of technical debt on the capacity and velocity of teams and organizations: viewing team and organization capacity as a portfolio of real options. In: Proceedings of the 4th International Workshop on Managing Technical Debt, pp. 28–31. IEEE (2013)
14. Shriver, R.: Seven strategies for technical debt (2011). http://ryanshriver.files.wordpress.com/2013/01/sevenstrategiestechnicaldebt.pdf
15. Yin, R.: Case Study: Planning and Methods, 4 edn., 248 p. Bookman, Porto Alegre (2010)
16. Kruchten, P.: What colour is your backlog? Agile New England (2012). http://pkruchten.files.wordpress.com/2012/07/kruchten-110707-what-colours-is-your-backlog-2up.pdf
17. Seaman, C., Guo, Y.: Measuring and monitoring technical debt. Adv. Comput. **82**, 25–46 (2011)
18. Beck, K., et al.: Manifesto for agile software development. http://www.agilemanifesto.org
19. Falessi, D., Kruchten, P., Nord, R.L., Ozkaya, I.: Technical debt at the crossroads of research and practice: report on the fifth international workshop on managing technical debt. ACM SIGSOFT Softw. Eng. Notes **39**(2), 31–33 (2014)

ReTest: Framework for Applying TDD in the Development of Non-deterministic Algorithms

André A.S. Ivo[1]($\boxtimes$) and Eduardo M. Guerra[2]

[1] Centro Nacional de Monitoramento e Alertas de Desastres Naturais (CEMADEN),
São José dos Campos, SP, Brazil
andre.ivo@cemaden.gov.br
[2] Instituto Nacional de Pesquisas Espaciais (INPE), São José dos Campos, SP, Brazil
eduardo.guerra@inpe.br

Abstract. TDD is a technique traditionally applied in applications with deterministic algorithms, when you have a known input and an expected result. Therefore, the challenge is to implement this technique in applications with non-deterministic algorithms, specifically when several random choices need to be made during its execution. The purpose of this paper is to present the ReTest framework, a JUnit extension, that allows an extension of the TDD technique, to enable its use for the development of non-deterministic algorithms.

Keywords: TDD · Non-determinism · Tests · Framework · JUnit · Metadata · Code annotations

1 Introduction

TDD (Test-Driven Development) is a software development technique in which tests are developed before code in short and incremental cycles [1]. The technique proposes for the developer to create a new flawed test, and then, to implement a little piece of code, in order to satisfy the current test set. Then, the code is refactored if necessary, to provide a better structure and architecture for the current solution [2,3].

TDD is traditionally applied in applications with deterministic algorithms, when there is a known input and one expected result. The challenge becomes, the use of TDD in applications with non-deterministic algorithms, where from executions with the same input it is possible to obtain different valid results. This type of approach usually uses several calls to functions that generates pseudo-random numbers during the algorithm execution in order to represent random decisions. Although it is not possible to know exactly what the output will be, it is usually possible to check whether the output received is considered valid or not. This scenario is very common in the development of scientific software [4].

The following factors make it difficult to develop non-deterministic software using TDD: (a) the result of the same execution may be different for the same

© Springer International Publishing AG 2017
T. Silva da Silva et al. (Eds.): WBMA 2016, CCIS 680, pp. 72–84, 2017.
DOI: 10.1007/978-3-319-55907-0_7

inputs, which makes it difficult to compare with a return value; (b) obtaining a valid return for a test case execution does not mean that valid return will be returned on the next executions; (c) there are may be several random decisions and a variable number of such of decisions, making not viable the creation of Mock Objects [5,6] that return fixed results for these decisions; and (d) it is difficult to execute a previous failed test with the same random decisions made in its last execution.

The goal of this paper is to present an extension for the JUnit framework called ReTest, developed by the authors of this work, which allows an extension of TDD to enable its application for algorithms with non-deterministic characteristics. The main feature of ReTest is to allow a test case that receives a class responsible to generate pseudo-random numbers to be executed several times with different seeds, increasing the test coverage. From the result of these repetitions, the framework stores the seeds that generated failures and uses them in future tests, ensuring that a scenario where an error was detected in the past is executed again.

The paper is organized as follows: Sects. 2 and 3 give a brief introduction to TDD and JUnit; Sect. 4 presents the ReTest framework; Sect. 5 describes the use of ReTest in the context of TDD technique; and, finally, the conclusion and proposals for future work are presented in Sect. 6.

2   Test Driven Development (TDD)

TDD is a code development and design technique, in which the test code is created before the production code. There are several research reported by Guerra and Aniche (see [1]) that indicates that the use of TDD can improve the source code quality. One of the reasons for the popularization of TDD is its explicit mention as part of the agile methodology Extreme Programming (XP) [7], however today is widely use out of its context.

In TDD practice, the developer chooses a requirement to determine the focus of the tests, then writes a test case that defines how that requirement should work from the class client point of view. Because this requirement has not yet been implemented, the new test is expected to fail.

The next step is to write the smaller amount of code as possible to implement the new requirement verified by the test. At this point, the added test, as well as all other previously existing tests, is expected to run successfully. Once you have passed the tests, the code must be refactored so that its internal structure can be continuously evolved and improved. The tests help to verify that the behavior has not been modified during refactoring.

This cycle is performed repeatedly until the tests added verify scenarios for all expected requirements of the class. The TDD cycle is presented in Fig. 1 [2,3].

With the use of TDD, the design of the code is defined in cycles. The idea is that with each new test added, create a small increment of functionality compared to the previous ones. TDD technique is described in several books, such as "Test-Driven Development by Example", "Agile Software Development, Principles, Patterns, and Practices", "Growing Object-Oriented Software, Guided

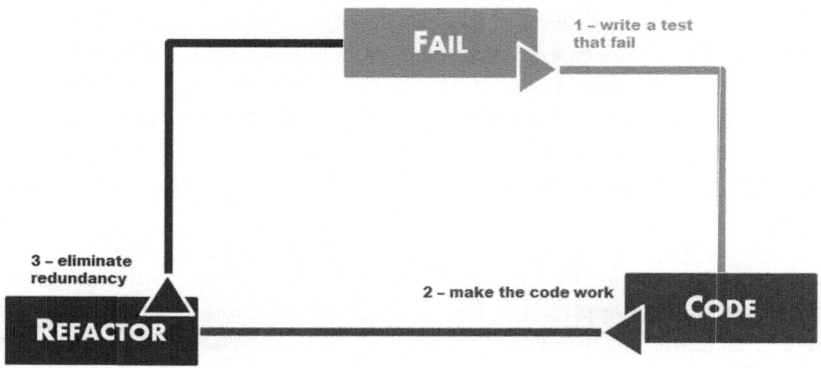

Fig. 1. TDD execution diagram

by Tests" and "Test-Driven Development: A Practical Guide" (see [2,3,8,9]), besides being widely used in industry.

3   JUnit Framework and Its Extension Points

JUnit is an open-source framework, created and developed by Erich Gamma and Kent Beck, for the creation of unit tests in the Java language. Its purpose is to be a basis for the creation of test automation code. It is widely used for the practice of TDD and its same model was used in the creation of test frameworks for other languages, being these frameworks referenced in general as XUnit. Some main features of such frameworks are the execution of test cases and the display of execution results [10].

JUnit, since version 4, provides extension points that allow the introduction of new functionality. Some of the most important JUnit extension points are represented by the classes Runner and Rule.

Runner is the class responsible for running the test methods from a test class. When a simple test class is executed with JUnit 4, it uses the class Block-JUnit4ClassRunner.class as the default runner. The Runner class hierarchy is represented in the diagram in Fig. 2.

In this way, to implement a Runner just create a new class and extend the Runner class shown in the diagram in Fig. 2.

To use just create a test project, and in the tests class include the annotation *@RunWith* and as argument pass the new class Runner.

This will replace all known JUnit 4 behavior. If you want to maintain the behavior, simply create a new Runner that extends the *BlockJUnit4ClassRunner* class.

Another extension point is known as Rule that other than Runner adds new behaviors mainly before and after the execution of each test. To write our own Rule, just create a class that implements the *TestRule* interface.

To use, just declare a public attribute in the test class and annotate it with *@Rule*, as shown in Code Snippet 1.

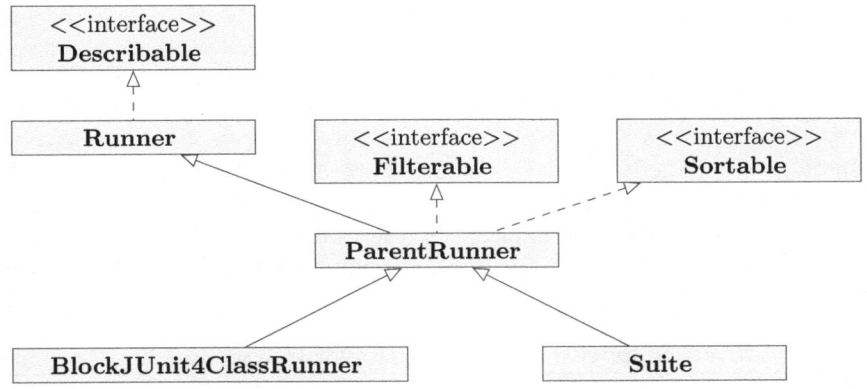

Fig. 2. Core class diagram of ReTest framework

Code Snippet 1. @Rule use example

```
public class TestClass {

  @Rule
  public NewRule newRule = new NewRule();

  public void testMethod(@RandomParam Random random){
    Object result = nonDeterministicAlgorithm(random);
    assertResult(result);
  }
}
```

In the example shown in Code Snippet 1, when executing the test project, who should call the *testMethod()* is newRule, responsible for adding the desired behaviors before and after the tests.

4   ReTest: Test Framework for Non-deterministic Algorithms

The ReTest framework, Random Engagement for Test, aims to extend JUnit to provide a framework for testing non-deterministic algorithms. It provides to its users a mechanism for managing the seeds used to generate random data in the algorithm being tested. Consequently, the same test can be repeated and the seeds used in failed runs can be repeated. These features facilitates the application of TDD for the development of non-deterministic algorithms. The ReTest framework is open-source and can be found at https://github.com/andreivo/retest.

4.1   Overview

To use ReTest the developer needs to create a test project using JUnit 4, and include the *@RunWith* annotation with *ReTestRunner.class* argument in the test class.

In the test methods the developer needs to include annotations to configure how it should be executed and annotations in the parameters that need to receive values generated and managed by the framework. The framework managed parameters are meat to be used as input data for the tests. The Code Snippet 2 shows a simple example of use.

Code Snippet 2. Simple example of how to use ReTest

```
@RunWith(ReTestRunner.class)
public class TestClass {

  @Test
  @ReTest(10)
  @SaveBrokenTestDataFiles(filePath = "/data/file1.csv")
  @LoadTestFromDataFiles(filePath = "/data/file1.csv")
  public void testMethod(@RandomParam Random random){
    Object result = nonDeterministicAlgorithm(random);
    assertResult(result);
  }
}
```

In the code shown in Code Snippet 2, the test method is marked with the *@ReTest(10)* annotation, which configures the framework to execute it 10 times. At each execution, the framework will initialize the parameter marked with *@RandomParam* received by the test method with a different seed. Notice that this object is passed as an argument to the method being tested, called *nonDeterministicAlgorithm()*. The class *Random* is used internally by the test method for the generation of its random numbers and, consequently, as a basis for its non-deterministic decisions. The *assertResult()* method used checks whether the return of the algorithm is considered valid. This test will be executed multiple times with Random initialized with different seeds, simplifying the execution of a large number of scenarios.

The seeds used in failed tests will be stored in the file "data/file1.csv", because the test method is marked with the *@SaveBrokenTestDataFiles* annotation. When executed again, in addition to the 10 repetitions configured by the *@ReTest* annotation, the test method will also run with the seeds stored in the "data/file1.csv" file, which is configured by the *@LoadTestFromDataFiles* annotation. That way, by running the failed tests again, you can check that the error has been corrected in addition to maintaining a set of regression tests.

Since in TDD the tests are executed frequently, throughout the development process the test executions should achieve good code coverage. This is reinforced by the fact that the tests that have failed previously are always executed again, creating data for regression tests.

4.2   Features

The ReTest framework has an API that allows you to:

(a) generate randomic data to be applied to the tests;
(b) create custom randomizers for data in the application domain;
(c) save the data from failed tests;
(d) save test data that has been successfully executed;
(e) save the return of the test method to generate a set of data based on random inputs and expected outputs;
(f) load test data from external files or sources;
(g) create custom mechanisms for handling external sources, both for saving and loading test data.

4.3   ReTest Annotation Set

In addition to the common JUnit annotations, the ReTest framework has a set of 4 annotations for the test methods and 4 annotations for the method parameters. The annotations for the methods are:

(a) **@ReTest:** This annotation is responsible for performing the test repetition. In this annotation it is possible to indicate how many times the test method should be executed;
(b) **@SaveBrokenTestDataFiles:** When you mark a method with this annotation, the input data will be saved to the file when the test fails;
(c) **@SaveSuccessTestDataFiles:** When you mark a method with this annotation, the input data will be saved to file when the test is successful;
(d) **@LoadTestFromDataFiles:** When you mark a method with this annotation, the input data from this file will be loaded and used in the execution.

The annotations for the method parameters are:

(a) **@IntegerParam:** Annotation indicates that the ReTest framework should pass as a parameter a random integer;
(b) **@RandomParam:** This annotation indicates that the framework should pass an instance of an object of type Random, with a known seed, so that it can be stored and retrieved from files, making it possible to reconstruct the same test scenario;
(c) **@SecureRandomParam:** This annotation indicates that the framework should pass an instance of an object of type SecureRandom, with a known seed, so that it can be stored and retrieved from files, making it possible to reconstruct the same test scenario;
(d) **@Param:** This annotation allows to indicate custom randomizers for the specific data types in the application domain, allowing the extension of the framework for random generation of several types of data.

4.4   Internal Architecture and Extension Points

This framework is based on the implementation of a new Runner, which reads and interprets the annotations presented in the session Sect. 4.3. The Fig. 3 shows the class diagram of the *ReTestRunner* implementation. In this diagram it is possible to observe the first extension point of the framework for personalization of the format of the data files, in the form of the implementation of the abstract class *TestDataFiles*. To configure the newly created class, it should be passed as a parameter to the *@SaveBrokenTestDataFiles*, *@SaveSuccessTestDataFiles*, and *@LoadTestFromDataFiles* annotations.

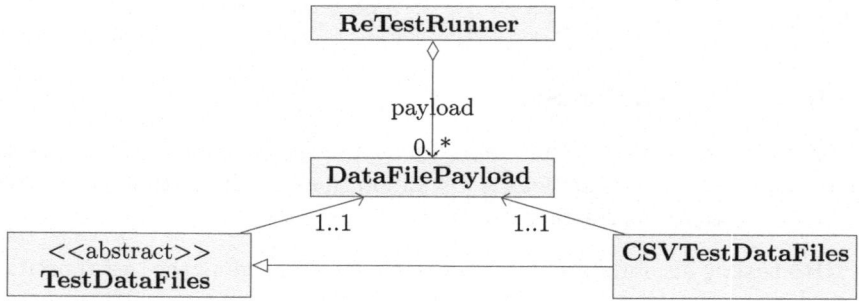

Fig. 3. Core class diagram of ReTest framework

The Fig. 4 shows the existing randomizers used to introduce parameters with random values in the test methods. At this point it is possible to observe the second extension point of the framework, in the form of the implementation of the abstract class *DataType*. To configure the new class created as the data generator for a test, it should be configure as an attribute of the *@Param* annotation.

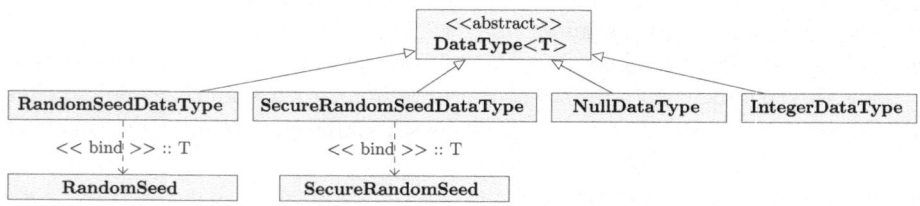

Fig. 4. Class diagram of randomized objects

5   TDD with ReTest

Because to the difficulties presented in the introduction of this article, TDD is not a technique normally used in the development of non-deterministic algorithms.

One of the goals of the ReTest framework is to make the use of this technique feasible for these scenarios.

From the use of ReTest is possible complement the development cycle of TDD as observed in Fig. 5. The steps of this new cycle consist of:

1. Create a new test that fails in at least one of its executions;
2. Store information of the failed scenarios to enable the verification if the changes in the production code make the failed scenario to pass;
3. Develop the simplest solution that makes the test suite run successfully for all inputs;
4. Run the test cases several times including new random generators with new seeds and with seeds that falied in previous test executions;
5. Refactor, if necessary, to provide a better internal structure for the final solution;

In this cycle, the steps of the original TDD are included, presented in Sect. 2. New steps were added as extensions proposed by the use of the ReTest framework, in order to ensure that TDD can be used as an application design technique and as a regression testing tool for non-deterministic algorithms.

To illustrate the use of this TDD cycle, consider the creation of a method to generate an array of "n" positions, with random numbers varying between 10 and −10, whose total sum of its elements is zero. This method receives as input parameter a Random object (used by the method to generate random numbers) and the size of the array to be generated.

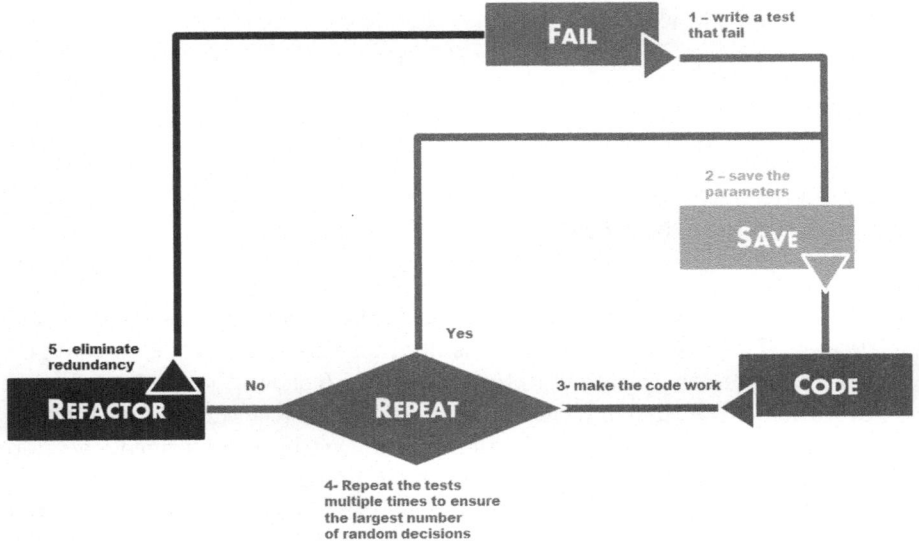

Fig. 5. Adaptation of TDD to ReTest

The following items describe the steps used to develop this function using TDD. Due to space limitations, the code for each of the steps will not be displayed and refactoring steps will be omitted.

(a) The first test asks the method to create an array with size 1. Since there is only one valid response for this case, which is 0, it is not necessary to use any ReTest annotations;

(b) It is written as the method implementation the return of a fixed value, and the test is executed successfully;

(c) The second test introduced invoke the method passing the parameter to create a size 2 array, initially checking only if the response has the appropriate array size. At first moment the test fails, because of the method in returning an array of size 1;

(d) As an initial implementation, an array of the size passed as a parameter is created and a random value generated within the range of -10 to 10 is set for each position;

(e) When executed, the tests pass, but it is known that the validity of the response is not being verified correctly;

(f) An auxiliary assertion method is then created to check the validity of the output according to the requirements. This method checks if the array has the expected size, if the value of each element is within range of -10 to 10, and if the sum of the elements is equal to zero, as shown in Code Snippet 3;

Code Snippet 3. Method for evaluating rules

```
private void assertElements(int[] arr, int arraySize) {
  int result = 0;
  //verify if all
  for (int i = 0; i < arraySize; i++) {
    assertTrue(arr[i] >= -10 && arr[i] <= 10);
    result = result + arr[i];
  }

  //verify the sum
  assertEquals(0, result);
}
```

(g) The test code for $n = 2$ is then modified so that it uses the assertion method created. The @ReTest annotation is used for this test method to configure the framework to execute it 10 times. The Fig. 6 shows the result of the test execution. Note that in 3 out of 10 scenarios the test runs successfully. As it is known that the implementation has not yet been performed, therefore the information about the failed test should not be saved yet;

(h) The code is changed so that the last array value is not randomly generated, but is the value that makes the sum to be equals to zero. The tests are run and now all pass successfully;

(i) The test is then annotated with @SaveBrokenTestDataFiles and @LoadTestFromDataFiles so that, from this point, that information of failed tests are stored and executed again, as can be seen in Code Snippet 4; From this point the test code for other methods is similar to this one, varying only the parameter "n" passed to the function *generateArrayWithSumZero()*;

Code Snippet 4. Example of test method

```
@Test
@ReTest(10)
@SaveBrokenTestDataFiles(filePath = "/tmp/dataTest.csv")
@LoadTestFromDataFiles(filePath = "/tmp/dataTest.csv")
public void test2(@RandomParam Random r) {
  int n = 2;
  int[] result = ArrayFactory.generateArrayWithSumZero(r, n);
  assertElements(result, n);
}
```

(j) The third test added uses as parameter n = 3, so that an array of size 3 is generated. This test already receives the *@ReTest* annotation to be repeated 10 times. When performing the tests, some of the repetitions fail, because in some cases this approach does not generate a valid response, as can be observed in Fig. 7;

(k) The TDD process follows by having all the test running in the 3-element array generation scenario, and then placing the annotations so that failed executions are stored and included in the regression tests;

(l) The process is repeated in the introduction of new tests with the parameter "n" assuming the values 10, 100 and 1000. Figure 8 shows the execution of the tests for an array with 1000 elements, after successive changes in the algorithm being developed;

From the example, it is possible to have a more concrete vision of how ReTest can be used to support the use of TDD in the development of a non-deterministic algorithm. Note that test cases are gradually being introduced and implementation is also occurring incrementally.

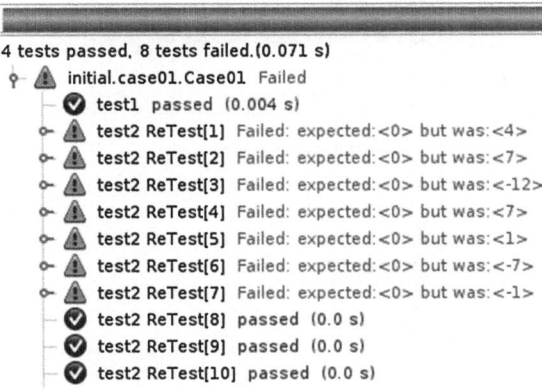

Fig. 6. Result of using ReTest for 2-position array

Fig. 7. Result of using ReTest for 3-position array with previous tests

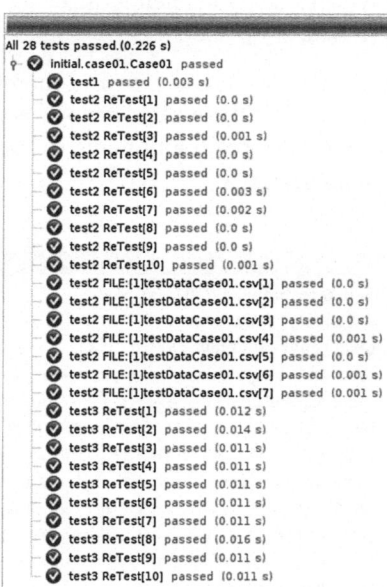

Fig. 8. Final result of the example with all tests running

The first point to emphasize is that when a test that needs to be repeated is executed, its execution is only considered correct when in all cases success is obtained. Note in Fig. 6, for example, that some executions always execute successfully, not because the implementation is correct, but because randomness leads to the correct solution in some cases. In this case, the repetition functionality of the framework is important because in each execution of the test suite it is possible to repeat the same test several times.

Another important point is in storing the seeds that generated failed test scenarios. Although it has not been commented, in the development of the example, in some cases modifications in code lead previous tests to fail in some scenarios. In this case, it was important to have the same test scenarios executing again to make sure that the problem was solved.

6 Conclusion

The goal of this work is to propose a test framework that facilitates the use of TDD for the development of non-deterministic algorithms. Some of the existing difficulties were to repeat exactly the same test cases flow that had failed previously and to be possible to have the test running successfully only in some executions. These difficulties are linked to the random decisions made during the execution of these algorithms.

The use of the ReTest framework makes it possible to use TDD for this type of algorithm, since it can repeat the same test several times and manage the seeds in order to repeat the failed test scenarios. The example presented in Sect. 5 showed how these functions can help us to follow the TDD flow to incrementally develop these algorithms.

As future work, we will evaluate the use of this framework for the development of a real non-deterministic algorithm using TDD. In addition, it is also intended to conduct an experiment with several developers to evaluate if they can use TDD in this way to develop such kind of algorithm.

References

1. Guerra, E., Aniche, M.: Achieving quality on software design through test-driven development. In: Mistrik, I., Soley, R., Ali, N., Grundy, J., Tekinerdogan, B. (eds.) Software Quality Assurance, pp. 201–220. Elsevier Inc., Amsterdam (2016)
2. Beck, K.: Test-Driven Development by Example. Addison-Wesley, Boston (2002)
3. Astels, D.: Test-Driven Development: A Practical Guide. Prentice Hall, Englewood Cliffs (2003)
4. Floyd, R.W.: Nondeterministic algorithms. J. ACM **14**, 636–644 (1967)
5. Mackinnon, T., Craig, P., Freeman, S.: Endotesting: unit testing with mock objects. In: Succi, G., Marchesi, M. (eds.) Extreme Programming Examined, pp. 287–301. Addison-Wesley Longman Publishing Co., Redwood City (2001)
6. Freeman, S., Mackinnon, T., Pryce, N., Walnes, J.: Mock roles, objects. In: Companion to the 19th Annual ACM SIGPLAN Conference on Object-oriented Programming Systems, pp. 236–246. ACM (2004)

7. Beck, K.: Extreme Programming Explained. Addison-Wesley Professional, Boston (2004)
8. Martin, R.: Agile Software Development, Principles, Patterns, and Practices. Prentice Hall, Englewood Cliffs (2002)
9. Freeman, S., Pryce, N.: Growing Object-Oriented Software, Guided by Tests. Addison-Wesley Professional, Boston (2009)
10. Beck, K., Gamma, E.: JUnit test infected: programmers love writing tests. In: Dwight Deugo, pp. 357–376. More Java Gems (2000)

Validation Board: Invalidating Ideas and Discovering the Problems that Must Be Solved

Avelino F. Gomes Filho$^{(\boxtimes)}$, Carlos F. Cardoso de Resende, Patrick S. Gazaneo, Vinicius Bittencourt, Raphael Duarte Paiva, and Rodrigo de Toledo

Postgraduate Program in Informatics,
Universidade Federal do Rio de Janeiro (UFRJ), Rio de Janeiro, Brazil
{avelino.filho,patrick.gazeano,vinicius.bittencourt}@ppgi.ufrj.br,
{cfc,rdpaiva}@ufrj.br, rtoledo@dcc.ufrj.com
http://www.ppgi.ufrj.br

Abstract. Project-Based Learning (PBL) is a teaching method used in many Computer Science courses. To implement it, it is necessary to choose good problems that will drive students' learning. These problems have to instigate students interest, encourage collaboration and help them to develop their knowledge of course-related topics. This paper presents a case study that sought to verify how the Lean Startup Idea Invalidation process applied with a Validation Board a business strategy assessment tool may assist in the choice of significant problems. Initial results indicate that this method helps students discard bad ideas, improve on the most interesting ones and choose products that are actually used by real users.

1 Introduction

Project-Based Learning (PBL) is a teaching method that promotes learning through experience. It allows students not only to learn the contents of courses but also to develop reasoning strategies for problem solving [1].

Unlike traditional teaching methods, in which the teacher conveys contents of the course and the students receive them without much questioning, PBL aims to engage students in the whole learning process, since the conception of the problem that will drive learning until its conclusion [1,12].

For this method to be feasible, it's necessary to determine the problem that will drive learning, which will be solved by students through a project. Such problems must have some characteristics: be challenging so that the students will explore the content of the course to reach a solution; be compatible with the level that the students are at; be open, with multiple paths to solution; be mutable as students acquire knowledge to solve them; not let students know if they made "the right decision"; generate interest and controversy that allow students to question what they are learning; stimulate collaboration and reasoning; have content related to the course [21].

© Springer International Publishing AG 2017
T. Silva da Silva et al. (Eds.): WBMA 2016, CCIS 680, pp. 85–97, 2017.
DOI: 10.1007/978-3-319-55907-0_8

Course-related concepts are researched, presented and discussed as it becomes necessary to use them to solve part of the problem. The teacher facilitates learning so these concepts become necessary during the period [11].

Selecting these problems is not a trivial task. With that in mind, the teachers of the Agile Methods for Software Development course of the Computer Science program at the Federal University of Rio de Janeiro (UFRJ) have decided to apply Lean Startup techniques, covering from the suggestions of possible problems, to the lean construction of products, and making them available to real users.

This work describes the Idea Invalidation and Fail Fast techniques from Lean Startup [20], applied by means of a Validation Board [22]. They can be used to help teachers and students choose relevant ideas that provide driving problems to PBL. It also presents an evaluation of this method.

Section 2 of this paper presents the theoretical framework, briefly describing the main concepts related to this research and other contributions to the theme. Section 3 describes the Validation Board, a tool used to invalidate ideas during the course. Section 4 presents the product evaluation metrics used by students to verify the users' acceptance of the products made available. Section 5 describes the method used in the research, its context and limitations. Section 6 presents and discusses the results. Finally, Sect. 7 concludes this work and directs future researches.

2   Theoretical Framework

2.1   Project-Based Learning (PBL)

The main objectives of PBL are increasing student engagement in the learning process and helping them develop a profound understanding of important concepts for the community they are part of. It is based on Situated Learning [13], in which students engage in problems they perceive as being important and similar to tasks performed by professionals [12,15].

Beside the characteristics described in the introduction, the guiding question (problem) should be feasible for students to investigate it and answer it, meaningful to promote learning, important, not trivial, contextualized in the real world, interesting and thrilling for students, and, above all, ethical [12].

Another relevant characteristic is that the method must follow a process similar to scientific research and Agile Software Development. Students explore the problems using new ideas, validating knowledge, producing results and exchanging information the whole time. Collaboration supports the process of investigating problems and builds the shared meaning of ideas [12].

2.2   Lean Startup

In our Computer Science course, one of the topics presented to the students is Lean Startup. The objective is to help students develop the ability to synthesize, apply, evaluate, discard and perfect solutions with the least possible effort [5].

Lean Startup was created from concepts developed by Ries [20]. It combines Agile Software Development with Client Development techniques and Toyota's Lean Production System, creating a strategy to develop products and services using the least possible amount of resources [16].

According to Ries [20], startups have high propensity to fail. The author writes that more important than developing a big plan that attempts to predict all possible risks is to carry out short, iterative experiments, preferably involving the target-audience directly. To the author, it is better that failures are identified quickly (Fail Fast), because this means that the company did not spend much time and money on something that would not work.

Besides failing fast, it is important to understand what went wrong. For Ries, it is very important that the experiences always generate learning that can be used to improve on a good idea and discard bad ones.

2.3   Related Work

In the literature it is common that the problems that will be solved by the students in a PBL context are previously chosen by the teachers or an expert [9,10,23]. However, some authors advocate that students should be involved since the beginning of the project and the teachers should act as facilitators and not as decision makers [8].

Münch [18] writes about the Validate Learning Cycle (Sect. 3) and the importance of development team discover the right problem before the project start. The author do not describes any tool or strategy to help the implementation of the cycle.

A contribution a little closer to the theme of this work is done by Pompermaier, Prikladnicki and Cauduro [19] describe how the use of Business Model Canvas (BMC), another tool for business strategy verification and assessment, can assist in the creation of startups. Like the present work, the authors stress the importance of understanding the problem and how this relates to possible clients. They describe how assessment methods (Subsect. 3.2) using BMC can help not only verify the usefulness of an idea, but also sell it to possible investors.

Another relevant piece of research on this theme is the one carried out by D'Alençon and Müller [3]. The authors studied the behavior of users of an education-related startup and how Pirate Metrics (Sect. 4) can be used to help companies make decisions. The results they obtained will be referred to when discussing the present work.

3   Validation Board

In order to improve the experimentation and learning process, the Validation Board [22] was conceived to help the implementation of the Validate Learning Cycle [20] and avoid waste of time, effort and money.

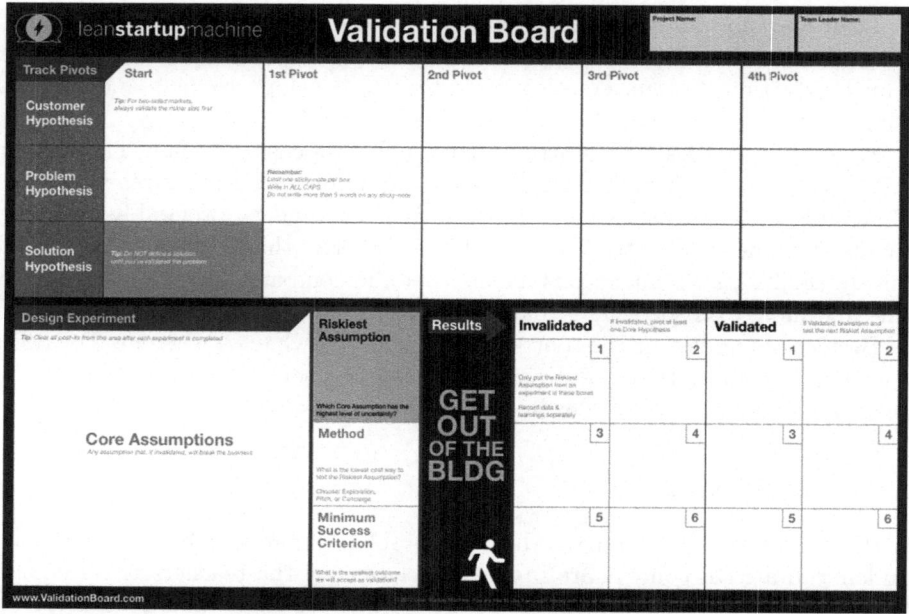

Fig. 1. Validation board. Source: [22]

The Validation Board consists in creating hypotheses about the problem, customer and solution, and setting experiments to be run, as in the model in Fig. 1. Through iterative experimentation, results about the validation or invalidation of a hypothesis are obtained.

The information stored on the board should help the entrepreneur make decisions. The following subsections describe how the Validation Board works in more detail, explaining each part of the board.

3.1   Track Pivots

Track Pivots is the section in the Validation Board where the experiment's hypotheses are described. They take three perspectives into account. The first is that the Problem exists (Problem Hypothesis). The second is that there are customers affected by the problem (Customer Hypothesis). The third is that the idea creates a solution for the customer to solve the problem (Solution Hypothesis). In the first iteration, the client's perspective is not filled out, because its goal is to confirm that there are potential clients affected by the problem imagined by the entrepreneur.

After the initial experiment, the pivoting stage begins. On the Validation Board, a pivot occurs when a hypothesis is invalidated, that is, either the supposition does not correspond to reality or there are other companies promoting very similar solutions. Some forms of pivoting are listed below [20].

Zoom-in Pivot: what was initially imagined as the functionality of a product becomes the product itself. Zoom-out Pivot is the opposite: the product with a given functionality is expanded in order to respond to other customer needs.

Client Segment Pivoting: the product attracts real customers, but not the ones imagined as the hypothesis in the customer's perspective. In other words, it solves a real problem, but needs to be placed in a different customer segment, for which the product had not been initially conceived. Pivoting for What the Customer Needs occurs when the customer's feedback indicates that the solution does not solve the customer's problem in a satisfactory way. This type of pivoting seeks to modify the solution so that it really solves the problem.

Business Architecture Pivoting is also possible. There are two main business architectures: high margin with low volume, or low margin with high volume. Another strategy can be Revenue Model Pivoting, which refers to the monetization or revenue model. Modifying the way in which revenue is generated can be one of the success factors for a startup. Often, there is no problem with the product developed or the proposed solution, but rather with the way in which the customer is being charged for using the product/service provided by the startup.

Technology Pivoting: sometimes, a startup finds a way to achieve the same solution using a completely different technology. This is relevant if the new technology can offer better price and/or performance to improve the startup's competitiveness in the market where it operates.

3.2   Design Experiment

In the Design Experiment section are the experiments that will test the ideas. This area is composed by the following boards: Core Assumptions, Riskiest Assumption, Assessment Method, and Minimum Success Criterion.

The Core Assumptions are related to the assumption perspectives, and should be validated through experiments. If they are invalid, the hypothesis must be pivoted or the idea must be discarded.

Among all the core assumptions, it is critically important to identify the Riskiest Assumption to be tested in the iteration. If this assumption is invalid, it has the biggest probability of "breaking" the business. As in the scientific process, a method is required to test the Riskiest Assumption. Some of the methods are described below.

The Exploration method has the goal of gathering a large amount of data about a given sector or customer, seeking to learn about the business. It can be implemented by means of surveys or interviews.

The Pitch method seeks to validate customer hypotheses. At this stage, one has an idea about how to solve the problem, and the goal is to find out whether the customers are willing to use it. The method consists of presenting the proposed idea to solve a problem via a short video or a brief presentation, and receiving customer feedback.

Minimum Viable Product (MVP) is the product built with the minimum amount of functionalities that is able to assess the assumption being tested.

When the evaluator builds the MVP, creating a way to gather usage metrics for the product and customer feedback is essential. A variation of this method is MVP Concierge, in which only the interface is built, while all of the back-end, which seems to be automatic, is actually run by people.

Regardless of the method, it is important to define the Minimum Success Criterion, which is the minimum value that must be obtained in the experiment for it to be considered valid. This number is an expectation based on market information. For example, it could be the number of users using the product, or the number of downloads. Predetermining the criterion avoids self-sabotage with Vanity Metrics, that is, believing that an unsatisfactory performance is able to validate an assumption [16,20].

3.3   Results

After defining the hypotheses, assumptions, method and goal, one must "get out of the building" and carry out the experiment. The last part of the board is for Results. At every iteration, the evaluated assumptions are recorded and classified as validated or invalidated.

4   Product Usage Metrics

When the first version of the product is made available, it is important to collect metrics in order to know if it is actually being used, and how the customers behave in relation to the product. For companies that develop software made available through the internet, such as websites, portals and Software as a Service, an interesting metrics for the product is AARRR [17].

Also known as Pirate Metrics, AARRR is an acronym for the stages customers go through when using a product. It stands for: Acquisition, indicating that the user reached the product for the first time. The user could sign up or start to use it right away. It is considered as usage when the user accesses some pages and uses the services for a few minutes without leaving it. Activation indicates that the user is returning to the website or service to use it. S/he visits more than one page or remains on the website for a long time. Retention occurs when the customer continues using the service for weeks or months. Referrals is when the customer, besides using the product, starts to recommend it to other people by e-mail, posts, messages, etc. and new users start using it as a consequence of those referrals. Finally, Revenue indicates how much the customer pays for using the service or to acquire the product.

These metrics behave similarly to a funnel, in the sense that many users go through the acquisition stage, but few acquisitions become revenue. The last column in Table 2 shows the estimations made based on McClure's [17] empirical experiments on the expected behavior of these metrics.

5   Research Method

5.1   Context of the Research

The Agile Methods course is offered as an optional course at the Computer Science program of UFRJ's Computer Science Department. It is a 4-credit course with 60 h of class. It has duration of one semester and has been offered once a year since 2011 [5, 7].

On the second class of the course, the students are invited to propose ideas through a brainstorming session for projects they will develop during the term. For each proposal, the students must describe the problem the product will solve and who the target audience will be. Then, the students are divided into groups of two or three. Each group of students chooses the ideas they wish to invalidate during the two following weeks.

After the students apply idea invalidation via the Validation Board, they present the filled out Validation Board, describing what they have assessed, how they did it, the pivots performed, and the results. The invalidated ideas are discarded, and the validated ones follow to the selection process. Here the students are invited to evaluate and choose only three problems, which will be turned into projects and used to learn Agile Methods for the rest of the term [5].

During the term, the students build the product and learn concepts related to Agile Methods. At the end of the term, they make their products available to real users and collect metrics related to software usage [5, 7].

5.2   Question and Assumptions

This research project intends to verify how the Idea Invalidation process through the Validation Board helps students choose real and relevant projects, which are able to promote the learning of Agile Methods. Its goal is to carry out initial analysis on how the Validation Board helps students find significant problems so that PBL can be used to teach Agile Methods.

The assumptions that help answer the research question are: A1: the Validation Board is able to invalidate bad ideas before the start of software implementation. A2: the Validation Board helps modify original ideas through pivoting. A3: when ideas are implemented and made available via software for potential customers, these ideas are indeed used by these customers. A4: students feel motivated with the problem they are solving and with the project they are building.

5.3   Method

The method chosen was Case Study [4]. The data collection method was divided into three parts. The first part refers to the beginning of the course, when the students used the Validation Board to invalidate ideas. The second part of the evaluation is Metrics Collection, as described in Sect. 4. This collection takes two weeks and is carried out after the product is made available for real users and before the start of the holidays. The metrics are part of the students' evaluation. Finally, a form is sent out to all students to hear about their view of how the strategy is used.

Three classes were selected to take part in this study: 2014.1, 2015.1 and 2016.1. During these terms, the classes were followed by 15 observers: seven in 2014, four in 2015 and four in 2016. Two of these were present in all classes studied.

Moreover, a group of two students was selected to develop their end-of-course assignment using the Validation Board to choose the product they would develop, as a requirement for graduating. Differently from the Agile Method classes, this group had one year to develop the assignment, during which time they had to write a monograph and present their work to a panel. This group was monitored by two researchers for the length of their work.

The Validation Board Use stage sought to assess assumptions A1 and A2. To do that, the observers monitored the students during the brainstorming session and the presentation of the Idea Invalidation result. The following variables were observed: total number of students, number of 2-student groups formed, number of 3-student groups formed, number of ideas presented in the brainstorming session, number of ideas invalidated, and average number of pivot operations performed per group.

In the Metrics Collection stage, the observers assessed the Pirate Metrics (Sect. 4) seeking to verify assumption A3. In the initial planning, it was expected that the 9 groups formed in the course, three in each class, produced data that could serve as input for the research. This was not possible, though. Two groups in the 2014 class did not collect metrics adequately. One of the 2015 projects had as target audience the restricted group of restaurant managers. In the same class, one of the groups decided to develop a hardware and software product, and could not make it available for users [6]. In the 2016 class, the three projects were impacted by a shorter academic term because of the 2016 Rio Olympic Games.

Therefore, two groups participated in the study: a group that developed *Caronas* in 2014.1, and a group that developed *Concurseiros* in 2015.1. The first is a website through which UFRJ students, teachers and employees can arrange car rides to commute to and from the university. *Concurseiros* is a website for people who take standardized tests for public jobs in Brazil, who can enter their grades and create a non-official ranking as soon as the official answers are published.

This evaluation stage also included the team that was developing the end-of-course assignment, which developed CookNow, a website with inverted recipes that helps people learn new recipes based on the ingredients they have at home.

The results were collected via Google Analytics (https://analytics.google.com). Since none of the projects was selling a product or service, the Revenue stage was not assessed. The group responsible for *Caronas* was unable to collect metrics related to Referrals.

Finally, in relation to assumption A4, on students' perception of the use of the Validation Board, survey forms were sent out to all students. Apart from asking students to identify their term, the form included the questions described in Sect. 6.

5.4   Limitations

The issues with data collection described in Subsect. 5.3 represent a limitation to the historic validity of the research, since the analysis of initial data was later reduced in face of unforeseen interference [2]. Because the students have to learn about Agile Methods during the course, they have a limited time to use the Validation Board, which restricts the number of invalidations and discarded ideas.

Moreover, because this is a social study done in specific contexts, the generalization of its results is limited. Specific elements, such as the class, the teacher, the researchers and the location make the procedure as well as the study results very specialized [4]. The forms sent out are limited because it is impossible to assist the responder, to know how the responder will interpret the questions, and there is no guarantee that the form will be returned [4].

6   Results and Discussion

Table 1 presents the results obtained during the first stage of the study.

Table 1. Results of idea invalidation using the validation board

Variable	Class			Assignment
	20141.1	2015.1	2016.1	
Total students	19	20	20	2
2-student groups	2	2	1	1
3-student groups	5	4	6	–
Number of ideas presented in brainstorming	27	21	29	2
Number of ideas invalidated	20	15	25	1
Average of invalidated ideas	74,07%	71,43%	86,21%	50%
Average number of pivot operations performed by groups of 3 or groups of 2	0,7	0,98	1,3	4

The results collected in the first stage and presented in Table 1 show that the students were able to discard many ideas. The groups discarded up to 71% of the ideas they had suggested in the brainstorming session. These discards happen because hypotheses are invalidated: the potential client does not really have the problem imagined; there are existing tools to solve the problem; the number of potential customers is too low; the solution is too complex, among others.

The number of pivot operations helps describe the extent to which the students were able to use Idea Invalidation to improve the original idea presented in the brainstorming session. The results are relatively low. During the presentations, some students reported that they did not have enough time to invalidate some ideas. However, it can be noticed that the team working on the end-of-course assignment, which had more time, was able to pivot more and improve on the original idea. This corroborates the restriction indicated in Subsect. 5.4.

Table 2 presents the results of the second evaluation stage. On this table, the last column presents the estimations ranges from McClure's experiments (Sect. 4) in order to better discuss the results. It must be noted that the products were promoted by the students through different strategies, which likely affected the number of acquisitions they achieved. *Caronas* was promoted in discussion groups and Facebook pages used by the university students. *Concurseiros* was promoted through posts in websites dedicated to the topic and in test locations where the selection exams for the Brazilian Marines took place in May of 2015. CookNow was promoted through two campaigns using Facebook Ads (https:// ads.facebook.com) and posts on student groups in social networks.

Table 2. Results of metrics collected after product implementation

Stage	Caronas		Concurseiros		CookNow		McClure's estimation
	Users	%	Users	%	Users	%	%
Acquisition	1542	71	3121	77, 04	5139	81, 23	70
Activation	109	7,07	549	17,59	798	15, 52	2 a 5
Retention	18	1,17	63	2, 02	217	4, 22	2 a 3
Referral	–	–	18	0, 57	114	2, 21	1 a 2

Regarding the metrics collected, we can see that the ideas and the products built by the students were well accepted by part of the users. In the Activation and Retention stages, the averages of all products were above McClures [17] estimations. In relation to the Referral stage, it is likely that the promotion of CookNow through Facebook and Facebook Ads significantly increased the number of referrals. Compared to the figures collected by D'Alençon and Müller [3], the numbers obtained in the stages are relatively lower: Activation (18.57%), Retention (11.98%). However, their research involved a real startup which, at the time, had more than 10 million accesses and had received financial investment. Even so, the Activation percentages are close to the ones obtained by *Concurseiros* and CookNow.

Table 3 presents the results of the forms collected. They were sent out to the 59 students that took the three courses, and were filled out by 27 of them (45.76%). From these, 7 are from the 2014 class, 13 are from the 2015 class, and 7 are from 2016. The questions were: (Q1) The Validation Board was able to help me invalidate ideas; (Q2) The Validation Board was able to help me pivot

Table 3. Results of the survey filled out by the students

Question	Strongly agree	Agree	Indifferent	Disagree	Strongly disagree
Q1	10	16	0	1	0
Q2	9	15	2	1	0
Q3	12	10	3	2	0
Q4	11	15	0	0	1
Q5	10	7	5	5	0

ideas; (Q3) The problem we solved through the project was encouraging; (Q4) I was able to learn Agile Software Development Methods through the project; and (Q5) If I could, I would give continuity to the project. All of the options followed the Likert scale [14].

Looking at the results, we can see that the respondents perceived the Validation Board as a tool that helped them discard ideas (96.30%) and saw the tool as something that can help them improve their ideas (88.89%). They observed that the problem they chose was encouraging (81.48%) and that the project helped them learn the content of the course (96.30%). Also, more than 62.96% of the students would like to continue their work.

7   Conclusion and Future Work

This work intended to verify how Idea Invalidation using the Validation Board can help select problems to be used in Project-Based Learning. Besides PBL, it also presented concepts related to Lean Startup, Validation Board and Software Use Metrics, specifically the Pirate Metrics.

Through the case study carried out, we were able to verify that the tool seems to help discard ideas that are not relevant (A1) and help choose those that solve problems perceived by real users (A3). The students felt that invalidating ideas via the Validation Board helped them choose an encouraging problem which they appreciated as part of the learning of Agile Methods (A4). Given the lack of other studies for comparison, the short time available, and the impact that the time variable may have had on idea improvement through pivoting, it was not possible to verify the validity of (A2).

This study will benefit from further research with future classes, especially giving more emphasis to metrics collection. It would also be interesting for some of these projects to continue being developed, in order to verify whether using the Validation Board produces better results with time. Moreover, applying this study outside of the academic context, in real startups, would be a further contribution.

References

1. Blumenfeld, P.C., Soloway, E., Marx, R.W., Krajcik, J.S., Guzdial, M., Palincsar, A.: Motivating project-based learning: sustaining the doing, supporting the learning. Educ. Psychol. **26**(3–4), 369–398 (1991). http://dx.doi.org/10.1080/00461520.1991.9653139
2. Campbell, D.T., Stanley, J.C.: Experimental and Quasi-Experimental Designs for Research. R. McNally, Chicago (1966)
3. D'Alençon, C.P.P., Müller, C.J.: Modelo de medição de desempenho para startup de saas: um estudo sobre a aplicação do modelo aarrr. Lume/UFRGS **1**(1), 1–24 (2015)
4. Gil, A.C.: Estudo de Caso: Fundamentação Científica, Subsídios Para Coleta e Análise de Dados e Como Redigir o Relatório. Atlas, São Paulo (2009)
5. Gomes Filho, A.F.: Modelo de Ensino baseado nos Métodos Ágeis de Desenvolvimento de Software. Informática, Universidade Federal do Rio de Janeiro, Rio de Janeiro (2016)
6. Gomes Filho, A.F., de Resende, C.F.C., Iglesias, C.A.F., Mayworm, J.G., Jardim, M.E.O., Paiva, R.D., de Toledo, R.: Agile software development learning through open hardware project. In: Proceedings of the 6th Workshop Brasileiro de Métodos Ágeis, pp. 1–8. IEEE, New York (2015)
7. Gomes Filho, A.F., de Resende, C.F.C., de Toledo, R.: Usando métodos ágeis para ensinar métodos ágeis. In: Anais do 5 Workshop Brasileiro de Métodos Ágeis, pp. 1–12. INPE, São José dos Campos (2014)
8. Helle, L., Tynjälä, P., Olkinuora, E.: Project-based learning in post-secondary education - theory, practice and rubber sling shots. High. Educ. **51**(2), 287–314 (2006). http://dx.doi.org/10.1007/s10734-004-6386-5
9. Herreid, C.F., Schiller, N.A.: Case studies and the flipped classroom. J. Coll. Sci. Teach. **42**(5), 62–66 (2013)
10. Hmelo-Silver, C.E.: Problem-based learning: what and how do students learn? Educ. Psychol. Rev. **16**(3), 235–266 (2004)
11. Kolb, D.A., Boyatzis, R.E., Mainemelis, C.: Experiential learning theory: previous research and new directions. In: Sternberg, R.J., Zhang, L. (eds.) Perspectives on Thinking, Learning, and Cognitive Styles, pp. 227–248. L. Erlbaum Associates, Mahwah (2001)
12. Krajcik, J.S., Blumenfeld, P.C.: Project-based learning. In: The Cambridge Handbook of the Learning Sciences, pp. 317–334. Cambridge University Press, Cambridge (2006). Chap. 19
13. Lave, J., Wenger, E.: Situated Learning: Legitimate Peripheral Participation. Cambridge University Press, Cambridge (1991)
14. Likert, R.: A technique for the measurement of attitudes. Arch. Psychol. **22**(140), 55 (1932)
15. Mahnic, V.: Teaching scrum through team-project work: students' perceptions and teacher's observations. Int. J. Eng. Educ. **26**(1), 96–110 (2010)
16. Maurya, A.: Running Lean: Iterate from Plan A to a Plan That Works. O'Reilly, Sebastopol (2012)
17. McClure, D.: Validation board. http://500hats.typepad.com/500blogs/2007/06/internet-market.html (2007). Acesso 29 July 2016
18. Münch, J.: Evolving process simulators by using validated learning. In: Proceedings of the International Conference on Software and System Process, pp. 226–227. IEEE Press (2012)

19. Pompermaier, L., Prikladnicki, R., Cauduro, F.: Startup garagem: Um programa de desenvolvimento de empreendedores. In: Anais da 25 Conferncia ANPROTEC, pp. 1–15. Cuiabá (2012)
20. Ries, E.: The Lean Startup: How Today's Entrepreneurs Use Continuous Innovation to Create Radically Successful Businesses. Crown Business, New York (2011)
21. Stanford University: Problem-based learning. Speaking Teach. **11**(1), 1–8 (2001). http://www.ncbi.nlm.nih.gov/pubmed/22139779
22. The Startup Machine: Validation board. https://www.leanstartupmachine.com/validationboard/ (2014). Acesso 24 July 2015
23. Tran, S.T., Le Ngoc Thanh, N.Q.B., Phuong, D.B.: Introduction to information technology. In: Proceedings of the 9th International CDIO Conference (CDIO) (2013)

IBM Design Thinking Software Development Framework

Percival Lucena[✉], Alan Braz, Adilson Chicoria, and Leonardo Tizzei

IBM Research, Sao Paulo, Brazil
{plucena,alanbraz,acjardim,ltizzei}@br.ibm.com

Abstract. The importance of understanding end user needs and involving them in the software development process is well known in software engineering. Agile Software Development methodologies have incorporated user feedback in different ways. User stories should represent the needs of a user, but often express the views of the Product Owner or the software development team. Several works have investigated integrating User Centered Design into Agile Software Development to satisfy end user needs. This work proposes a different approach focused on satisfying end user needs employing Design Thinking iterative software development. This methodology was applied in five real software development projects which have been analyzed as part of this work.

Keywords: IBM Design Thinking · Agile Software Development · Scrum

1   Introduction

Agile Software Development (ASD) has improved software delivery process through the use of short and fast iterations. By simplifying software engineering practices agile methodologies were able to achieve a higher success rate than traditional waterfall projects [1]. The Agile Manifesto emphasizes the collaboration with customers, but its approach does not guarantee that the software development team will work towards solving the correct problem [2].

Software development projects have a higher chance to solve the right problem when focused on satisfying users needs [3]. Agile methods including Scrum have already tried to follow this approach by incorporating user feedback as part of the requirement process. Cohn [4] has introduced a Customer Team that performs brainstorming sessions to write user stories that capture all the facets of user needs. The author also proposes to adopt observation techniques, conduce user interviews, apply questionnaires, create personas and develop user interfaces prototypes.

Although user stories can help understand the problem that needs to be solved, several agile development projects adopt a simpler requirements gathering process defined by a single Product Owner (PO) who might represent the view of different project stakeholders but not necessarily the end-users needs,

© Springer International Publishing AG 2017
T. Silva da Silva et al. (Eds.): WBMA 2016, CCIS 680, pp. 98–109, 2017.
DOI: 10.1007/978-3-319-55907-0_9

desires and aspirations. Under these conditions, the developer team implements a limited solution for the problem described at the Product Backlog [5].

Design Thinking (DT) [6] offers an innovative way of thinking based on divergence and convergence around the real users in order to understand their intentions and motivations and how to tackle everyday problems. This collaborative way of work allows empowered development teams to make better decisions, quickly test ideas with the user including feedback as a fundamental piece of the solution process.

IBM Design Thinking [7] extends the original DT method providing a new approach to write requirements, organize teams, and track project progress including end-user feedback during all the project development phases. A problem for the reader willing to learn about IBM Design Thinking is that most information about it is scattered over various documents and videos. Furthermore, neither these documents and videos nor existing DT literature qualitatively assesses the usage of IBM Design Thinking as software development framework. The two main contributions of this paper are the following: (i) to provide a compact and easy-to-access description of IBM Design Thinking and its differences to DT; (ii) to assess strengths and limitations of using IBM Design Thinking as an ASD based on a survey with developers and designers of five real software development projects.

The rest of this paper is divided as follows: Sect. 2 presents an introduction to Design Thinking. Section 3.1 presents IBM contributions to DT as an software development framework. Section 4 presents a survey about projects that have adopted IBM Design Thinking SDF. Section 5 presents related works. Section 6 presents a brief discussion of the survey results. Finally, Sect. 7 presents conclusions and future work.

2   Background: The Design Thinking Process

According to Brown [8], Design Thinking is a methodology applied by project teams for innovation activities focused on satisfying user needs. DT is an abstraction of the mental process used by designers to create new ideas.

The analytic process pursued in science explores a solution for a given problem. DT approach allows exploration in both problem and solutions. The process

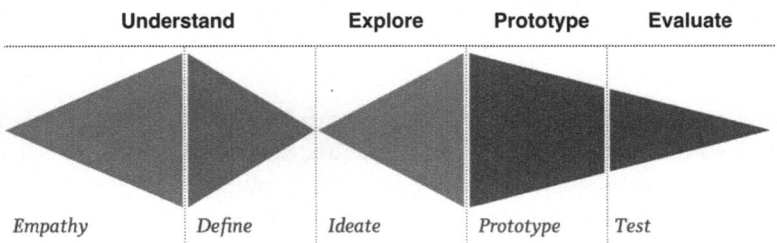

Fig. 1. Design Thinking Process - Adapted from [10]

requires diverging on many possible solutions and converging on a focused direction. Diverging phases such as Empathy and Ideate, diverge the problem space, while Understand, Prototype and Test phases converge to a solution. Figure 1 shows the main phases of the DT process.

Understand Phase: The first phase of DT process consists of the Empathy mode, a set of activities to help to understand the users, within the context of their problems. The first activity to be executed consists in observing how users interact with their environment. Scenarios are observed through user perspectives in order to capture the context of the project and understand user physical and emotional needs. Engaging with users through interviews and questionnaires provides a deep understanding about what they think and feel. The information gathered could be later translated into insights and ideas to solve user needs [9]. The Define mode of the process brings clarity and focus to the design space. Its goal is to craft a meaningful and actionable problem statement. The information gathered is then analyzed and summarized using tools such as personas and empathy maps.

Explore Phase focus on the generation of new ideas in order to avoid obvious solutions and thus increase the innovation potential. Brainstorming is a common technique used in this phase that offers diverging thoughts in a way to explore new ideas and solutions. The intention of brainstorming is to leverage the collective thinking of the group, by engaging with each other, listening, and building on other ideas [6].

Prototype Phase is the iterative generation of artifacts intended to answer questions to solve the design problem. Prototypes in DT are generally mock-ups that support the elaboration and evaluation of product concepts with the goal of finding out which ways are right or wrong. The goal of the prototype phase is to validate the ideas proposed during the Explore phase. The scope of a prototype should be limited. Storyboards can be used to develop scenarios [10].

Evaluate Phase solicits users for feedback about the prototype created. User Experience (UX) evaluation techniques could be used to test the prototype. Micro-tests are a common approach to evaluate prototypes online. The time available for recruiting end users, performing the tests, and for analyzing and reporting the test results is usually very short, but it provides quick responses for the development teams [11].

3   IBM Design Thinking Software Development Framework

The stated goal of industrial manufacturing processes is to achieve repeatability to minimize uncertainty. It can be implemented with well-defined specifications and acceptance criteria, robust and dependable tooling, and economies of scale. In a world of industrial manufacturing processes, this separation of design from engineering was considered desirable.

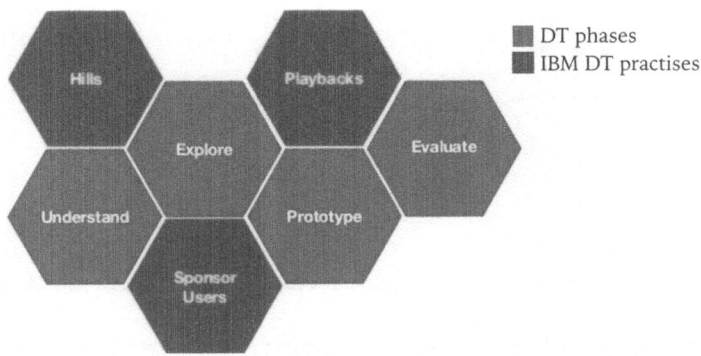

Fig. 2. IBM Design Thinking compared to traditional Design Thinking

Nevertheless software is built in the medium of code. Because of the uncertainty of the medium, software design and software engineering are intrinsically linked, codependent activities. While traditional DT often separates design from implementation, software demands close-knit, collaborative relationships between designers and engineers. Without including software engineers as a part of design the design team, a software project is likely to fail.

IBM Design Thinking Software Development Framework goal is to extend DT principles so they be applied to develop software that captures user needs at the speed and scale required for fast pace incremental software development such as on Cloud based software. While it shares some similarities with other Design Thinking methods, it has a few modifications, including three practises that are unique to the framework: Sponsor users, Playbacks and Hills [12]. The integration of those practises to Design Thinking are shown in Fig. 2.

3.1   IBM Design Thinking Roles and Workflow

The IBM Design Thinking defines three major roles with different set of responsibilities. The Product Manager is responsible for understanding the market opportunity and defining the product release. He is responsible for the project kick-off, defining and recruiting Sponsor Users, and defining the playback strategy. The Designer is responsible for the user experience and functional design. She is engaged in developing design artifacts, mock ups, user research and the design sprint plan. The engineering team is responsible for the technical design and implementation of the release. They are in control of project architecture and executable code, prototype and the technical sprint plan.

IBM Design Thinking Software Development Framework activities are divided into two main phases. The Visioning Phase is responsible to develop software requirements through the use of several Design Thinking practises that combines user personas, empathy maps, hills and story maps. The Delivery Wave consists of software development Sprints conduced by multidisciplinary teams that includes Sponsors Users, who contribute with constant feedback about the

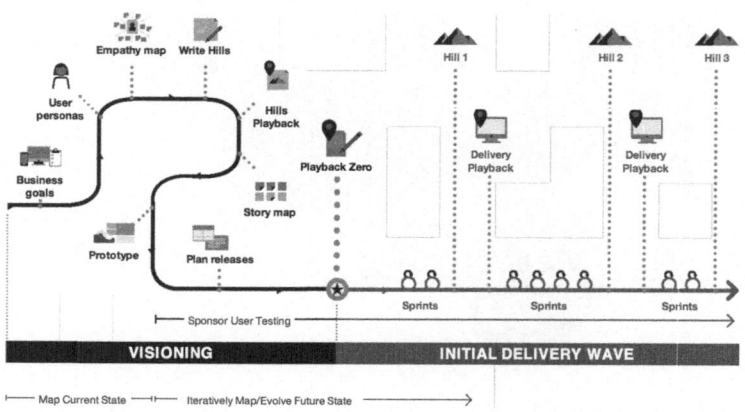

Fig. 3. IBM Design Thinking Software Development Framework

delivered artifacts. Figure 3 illustrates the workflow of a sample IBM Design Thinking project.

3.2 Hills

Hills introduce a new way to express users needs into project requirements. Each individual Hill articulates a clear goal and containable scope defined to be achievable in one release or in a finite set of releases. A Hill must be written to meet a specific, clearly-defined user problem that is informed by user research. Although the Hills are written from the customer's perspective, they also emphasizes important intersections between user expectations and business requirements. Hills are composed of three elements: a *who* that describes a user or a specific group of users; a *what* that describes a problem that needs to be solved; and a *wow* a measurable target for the Hill completion [7]. Table 1 illustrates a sample Hill.

Complex Hills can be decomposed into Sub-Hills. Those should be cohesive such as if released independently, providing value on its own. Sub-Hills can be further detailed by scenarios which provide perspectives of different Sponsor Users. A Foundation Hill is a set of hills that represent the Product backlog for a Iteration. In order to keep fast iterations, one should not select more that three hills for each Foundation Hill [13].

Table 1. Sample hill

Who	A sales leader
What	Can get insights from a specific market region
Wow	By receiving consolidated data information from all available sources

3.3   Sponsor Users

User archetypes like personas can represent only part of understanding user needs [14]. Participation with real users provides the remaining insights to improve user experience. A Sponsor User is a real human being who can share his or her experiences and point of view. Sponsor users can be selected among existing users of a product, or potential users for a new product. A good practice consist of selecting users who have extreme point of views and thus can contribute with non-trivial insights. Sponsor users will have a role somewhat similar to a PO on Scrum process, but will act by providing individual information about their real needs.

A Sponsor User makes a significant commitment of time. They will be involved in all product development phases. Sponsor Users will be interviewed by Product Management and Design team members early on in the project. They will also participate throughout the release process to review artifacts like Hills, Design prototypes, and project deliverables.

3.4   Playbacks

Playbacks are checkpoints when the project team and Sponsor Users meet in order to review the state of the project and plan next steps. Playbacks are a safe space to provide and receive feedback. Playbacks occurs at the end of each project development phase and have different goals.

Business Goals Playback establishes an initial market point of view and pre-liminary business case. The purpose of this meeting is to understand the users through user research practices, defining the main user needs and identifying Sponsor Users who will be able to develop the project Hills.

Hills Playback are a set of meetings involving the product team and Sponsor Users whose goal is to align on the three primary Hills of a release, or set of releases. The first Hill meeting should define the release strategy specifying the major Hills and their relationship in the product Roadmap. By the end of the Hills Playback meetings the team should be able to make a rough order-of-magnitude estimate of work to determine whether it can delivered within the time and resource constraints.

Playback Zero happens just before the hardcore delivery work begins. It is a time for the whole team and broader stakeholder community to commit to the user experience for the product. This meeting aligns the team around the finalized version of the Hills and the user experience to achieve them. Playback zero should use a Customer Journey Map [15] to provide a diagram of the Hills from an individual's perspective of his experience with the service or product which is being developed.

Hills are implemented in timebox iterations. A self-reliant multidisciplinary team is organized to implement each hill. During Playback Zero, the Product Manager defines a certain number of hours that could be invested on each Hill. Teams are fully empowered to achieve the Hills, within their investment parameters, and make the trade-offs required to hit the marks. A successful Playback

Zero should end with the team and stakeholders in agreement on the commitment to deliver each Hill.

Delivery Playbacks are meetings among the product development team and the Sponsor users to demonstrate a real working solution for a Hill. In cases where the proposed solutions do not match with technical feasibility, design and engineering team members collaborate to achieve feasible solutions. At the end of the Delivery Playback, the team should decide on whether to release the project to real users. Once the software is released, those users can be observed providing course-corrections as early as possible.

4   Design Thinking Survey

We have conducted a survey on how IBM Design Thinking was applied in real software development projects at IBM. The goal of our survey was to understand how those teams have applied DT on their projects by (i) identifying the practices adopted; (ii) identifying the project structure and phases and; (iii) understanding the project results achieved. This survey was designed based on the guidelines defined by [16] and it is cross sectional as participants were asked for information at one fixed point, which in this case was a two-week period.

We have created a questionnaire with open and closed questions, which was self-administered and is available at http://bit.ly/2a3qRr0. We have asked ten Product Managers and Software Architects responsible for software development projects to provide accurate information regarding IBM Design Thinking Framework usage on their projects. The sample of participants was chosen by convenience, since IBM Design Thinking is relatively new and thus few projects have used it. Table 2 provides a summary of the information gathered from the five survey responses received.

4.1   Design Thinking Survey Results

According to the ScrumAlliance's 2015 State of Scrum Survey the highest business priority for Scrum projects is to fulfill users needs [17]. Based on our survey responses, the extra effort spent on Design Thinking Visioning Phase has helped all the teams to have a deeper understanding of the problem to be solved. The Product Managers have reported that most of the end users confirmed that the solution delivered was valuable and satisfied their usage needs. We assume the time spent on Design Thinking Visioning Phase contributes positively to improve ASD goals and delivery results.

We have noticed that the up-front work phase on IBM Design Thinking projects were usually longer than other ASD projects. Nevertheless the percentage of time spent on Design Thinking Visioning Phase was smaller than 30% for all projects except for Project 1. The number of Sponsor Users involved did not influence the percentage of total project time spent on Visioning Phase as shown in Fig. 4.

Table 2. Design Thinking Survey summary

Proj1: sales portal	**Problem description:** Enterprise sales were not fully automated depending on spreadsheets and emails. The goal of the project was to develop an Enterprise portal for the customers of a telecommunication company
	DT usage: The project team has selected 6 Sponsor Users among the 3 biggest customers of the new portal. During 5 weeks, Sponsor Users were observed and interviewed. The project team developed empathy maps, as-is scenarios and identified major pain points and opportunities. The Sponsor Users helped to identify 3 Hills for the product development. The project team developed low-fidelity prototypes and Sponsor Users performed user testing. A multidisciplinary team composed of 6 persons including software engineers and designers detailed and developed the Hills sequentially in 6 weeks, with 2 intermediate milestones until the final product release
	Results: The Sponsor Users were involved in Delivery Playbacks participating in all product demonstrations. They have provided useful feedback, assuring the Hills satisfied their needs. The product released included the minimum viable product that attended Sponsor Users needs and was delivered faster than similar projects
Proj2: backup tool	**Description:** Backup and system maintenance were very complex tasks that required special training for the users
	DT usage: A few beta users of the existing product were selected as Sponsor Users for the new product release. Since those users were not available frequently, the project team has developed personas to represent them. The team wrote 3 Hills for the storage administrator persona. Delivery playbacks originated 2 beta releases. Sponsor Users revised the terminology, helped adjusting workflows, added messages, and changed panel texts
	Results: The new release allows users to learn about the product without leaving the GUI, which keeps them engaged when installing and using the product. Support help desk tickets have dropped more than 50%
Proj3: health care provider app	**Description:** The goal of the project was to create a mobile application for caregivers. The application should help professionals to manage schedules, keep information about elderly patients and deal with health plans paperwork
	DT usage: The project started with a Market Playback iteration. The Product Manager and a team composed by 25 dispersed members established a vision for the product based on user research. The team has selected 8 Sponsor Users including care workers from different customers and partners organizations. During the Hills Playback the team created empathy maps, story boards and as-is scenarios in order to understand the users. Playback Zero defined Caregivers' Hills as a first release and Child welfare workers' Hills as a second product release. The product was developed in 12 weeks through 4 iterations
	Results: Sponsor User feedback helped a geographically disperse team to be aligned to a single product vision. The team was focused on Sponsor Users feedback and was able to deliver a product faster than other distributed Agile teams in the company

Table 2. *(Continued)*

Proj4: AIX high availability	**Problem description:** System administrators liked to use a legacy command line tool, but did not have access to the logging information needed to perform their work
	DT usage: The project has spent 5 months on planning phase recruiting 16 Sponsor users who provided more than 162 hours of feedback. The project stakeholders expressed their needs into 10 hills. After the prioritizing phase, 3 Hills that represented the most important pain points were selected for the Foundation Hill. Next, the project team worked during 11 iterations producing 2 intermediary beta releases until the final product release
	Results: Users were excited with the new web based console because the UI was intuitive and it helped System Administrators to solve their most important daily problems without the need of contacting support
Proj5: visitors app	**Problem description:** In order to receive visitors in the company, employees had to access a cumbersome legacy database, making hard to arrange visits while out of the office. A new mobile application was developed to simplify the process
	DT usage: The project multidisciplinary team was composed by 7 software engineers and 2 designers. Two sponsor users were recruited among the application population and had defined 2 Hills in a process that took 3 weeks until Playback Zero. The software development adopted 1 week iterations and took 8 weeks until the final application release
	Results: All the surveyed users were very pleased with the mobile application that was released in the company internal application store. New visitors could be scheduled in a few seconds saving time for all the application users

Participants from Project 1 and Project 3 mentioned that managing Sponsor Users took them several hours every week. Since some of the Sponsor Users could not be available on the product demonstration sessions the teams have decided to record videos so they could receive feedback asynchronously afterwards. All the project teams surveyed agreed that Sponsor Users brought important insights for the product development.

5 Related Work

User Centered Design (UCD) and ASD share a common focus on users and customers. The two methodologies diverge on how to organize teams and the need for upfront project and design. UCD encourages the team to understand their users before the start of the product development, while ASD methods like Scrum and Extreme Programming are usually against an up-front investigation and documentation [18].

Common approaches to incorporate UCD in Agile methods include creating UX tasks as part of User Stories and set up a parallel Sprint so design teams

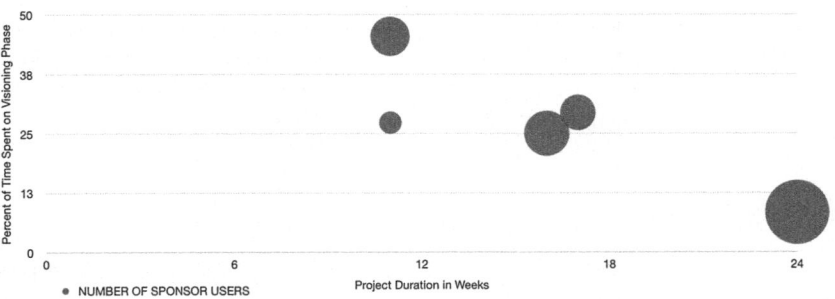

Fig. 4. IBM Design Thinking percent of time spent on Visioning Phase vs total time project duration vs number of Sponsor Users

can work one Sprint ahead of development teams [19]. Those approaches restrict user feedback since users are not directly involved in the software development process [20]. In order to improve end-user collaboration new Agile methodologies based on DT principles have been proposed including Lean UX, Design Sprints and IBM Design Thinking.

Lean UX is a fast user-centered software development framework based on principles from DT, ASD and Lean production. The Lean UX process aims to produce as quickly as possible and with the minimal resources a product that satisfies customer needs [21]. The development targets are specified at the start of each iteration. The iterative process begins by defining the assumptions and the problem. Then solution hypothesis are created for proto-personas. Next, sketching and ideation exercises produce a prototype that is further detailed on the following iterations to create a MVP (Minimum Viable Product). User micro-testing and interviews takes place every week when user representatives review the MVP [22].

IBM Design Thinking and Lean UX are both based on Design Thinking principles but differ on how to implement the process. Besides using personas, IBM Design Thinking incorporate Sponsor Users who provide feedback defining requirements Hills and also provide feedback and user testing during Delivery Playbacks.

Knapp [23] propose to create a Design Sprint to define strategic goals and define the product scope before the team starts to work on a software development project. A Design Sprint is a time-constrained framework that uses DT to help teams to create a new product, service or feature [24]. A Design Sprint consists of five discrete phases: *Understand*: discovers the business opportunity, the audience, the competition, the value proposition, and defines metrics of success; *Converge*: explores, develops and iterates creative ways of solving the problem, regardless of feasibility; *Diverge*: identifies ideas that fit the next product cycle and explores them in further detail through storyboarding; *Prototype*: designs and prepares prototypes that can be tested with users; *Test*: conducts user testing focusing on product's primary target audience.

Unlike Design Sprints IBM Design Thinking does not provide a single Design Sprint to understand the user research problem and provide a solution to a design problem but a framework where those activities are integrated as part of different Playback phases of the software development process.

6   Discussion

A known limitation of IBM Design Thinking process is related to the project team structure. The process can not be applied successfully if the company does not change their approach to solving problems. Similarly to the way IT departments had to reorganize to change from command and control Waterfall structures into Agile teams, implementing IBM Design Thinking also requires those teams to reorganize and review their work model and functional roles.

In order to implement the SDF successfully it is necessary to the create multidisciplinary teams composed by designers, engineers, product managers and users who work together to drive a vision of the software development. Fragmented teams can easily get out of the sync and important feedback may be lost under those conditions.

7   Conclusion

While in the past, a software potential market share was constrained in large part by the supply chain and distribution capability, today, the offering's growth is now determined by its fitness for user's needs. IBM Design Thinking brings up-front analysis and user feedback in all the iterations offering a better understanding of what problems need to be solved and what are the best solutions to satisfy the user needs.

According to our survey, using a likert scale varying from very low to very high, 80% of the surveyed reported End-Users had a very high satisfaction rate on the projects delivered. The user experience improvement was related to a productivity boost resulting in time and resources savings and user base growth for the delivered services. Albeit those qualitative results are promising further studies should be done in order to measure those satisfaction levels accurately and to comprehend the limitations of the software developed framework.

Acknowledgements. We would like to thank Marco Aurelio Stelmar Netto, Heloisa Candello and Miroslav Azis for reviewing this paper and for their constructive feedback.

References

1. VersionOne. Annual state of agile development survey (2016)
2. Norman, D.A.: The Design of Everyday Things: Revised and Expanded Edition. Basic books, New York (2013)

3. Marques, A.B., Cavalcante, E., Luiz, R.: Aplicando design thinking para melhorar a qualidade de um aplicativo movel. In: Brazilian Symposium on Software Quality (2015)
4. Cohn, M.: User Stories Applied: For Agile Software Development. Addison-Wesley Professional, Boston (2004)
5. Pichler, R.: Agile Product Management with Scrum: Creating Products that Customers Love. Addison-Wesley Professional, Boston (2010)
6. Brown, T.: Change by Design. Collins Business, New York (2009)
7. Azis, M.: IBM design thinking (2016a). http://www.ibm.com/design/thinking/
8. Brown, T., et al.: Design thinking. Harv. Bus. Rev. **86**(6), 84 (2008)
9. Plattner, H.: An Introduction to Design Thinking Process Guide. The Institute of Design at Stanford, Stanford (2010)
10. Lindberg, T., Meinel, C., Wagner, R.: Design thinking: A fruitful concept for it development? In: Meinel, C., Leifer, L., Plattner, H. (eds.) Design Thinking. Understanding Innovation, pp. 3–18. Springer, Heidelberg (2011)
11. Nielsen, L., Madsen, S.: The usability expert's fear of agility: an empirical study of global trends and emerging practices. In: Proceedings of the Nordic Conference on Human-Computer Interaction: Making Sense Through Design, pp. 261–264. ACM (2012)
12. Azis, M.: The making of IBM design thinking (2016b). http://ibm.co/1T8psiW
13. Gothe, M.: Adopting IBM design thinking for solution development (2016)
14. Chamberlain, S., Sharp, H., Maiden, N.: Towards a framework for integrating agile development and user-centred design. In: Abrahamsson, P., Marchesi, M., Succi, G. (eds.) XP 2006. LNCS, vol. 4044, pp. 143–153. Springer, Heidelberg (2006). doi:10.1007/11774129_15
15. Richardson, A.: Using customer journey maps to improve customer experience. Harv. Bus. Rev. **15** (2010)
16. Kitchenham, B.A., Pfleeger, S.L.: Personal opinion surveys. In: Shull, F., Singer, J., Sjøberg, D.I.K. (eds.) Guide to Advanced Empirical Software Engineering, pp. 63–92. Springer, London (2008)
17. ScrumAliance: State of Scrum - 2015 (2016)
18. da Silva, T.S., Silveira, M.S., Maurer, F.: Ten lessons learned from integrating interaction design and agile development. In: Agile Conference, pp. 42–49. IEEE (2013)
19. da Silva, T.S., Martin, A., Maurer, F., Silveira, M.S.: User-centered design and agile methods: a systematic review. In: AGILE, pp. 77–86. Citeseer (2011)
20. Bordin, S., Angeli, A.: Focal points for a more user-centred agile development. In: Sharp, H., Hall, T. (eds.) XP 2016. LNBIP, vol. 251, pp. 3–15. Springer, Cham (2016). doi:10.1007/978-3-319-33515-5_1
21. Liikkanen, L.A., Kilpiö, H., Svan, L., Hiltunen, M.: Lean UX: The next generation of user-centered agile development? In: Proceedings of the Nordic Conference on Human-Computer Interaction: Fun, Fast, Foundational, pp. 1095–1100. ACM (2014)
22. Gothelf, J., Seiden, J.: Lean UX: Applying Lean Principles to Improve User Experience. O'Reilly, California (2013)
23. Knapp, J., Zeratsky, J., Kowitz, B.: Sprint: How to Solve Big Problems and Test New Ideas in Just Five Days. Simon and Schuster, New York (2016)
24. Banfield, R., Lombardo, C.T., Wax, T.: Design Sprint: A Practical Guidebook for Building Great Digital Products. O'Reilly, California (2015)

SimKan: Training Kanban Practices Through Stochastic Simulation

Francisco Jose Rego Lopes[1](✉) and Fabio Petrillo[2]

[1] Universidade Estadual do Ceara (UECE), Av. Dr. Silas Munguba, 1700, Campus do Itaperi, Fortaleza, CE 60.714-903, Brazil
lopespaz@yahoo.com.br
[2] Instituto de Informatica, Universidade Federal do Rio Grande do Sul (UFRGS), Caixa Postal 15.064, Porto Alegre, RS 91.501-970, Brazil
fabio@petrillo.com

Abstract. Kanban is a software development methodology that has grown and gained more supporters. Proportional of this growth, dissemination of knowledge in the use of its practices is essential. Moreover, training in software processes is not always a trivial endeavour, and exploring some project practices in traditional training rooms can be a complex task. This paper proposes SimKan, an analogical serious game for training Kanban practices. SimKan uses stochastic simulation to introduce aspects of randomness in the game, allowing a quasi-true experience on Kanban, performing in a short time-frame and using simple tools. Our results show that SimKan is adequate to train teams in Kanban, bringing positive results in a short time-frame and with low cost.

1 Introduction

During the last decade, the use of agile software development methods has increased and become more popular [1]. Agile methodologies are no longer restricted to startups or small system developing companies, and the number of big companies adopting agile methodologies is increasing every year. One of the outstanding agile methodologies is Kanban [2].

Kanban is a scheduling and an inventory-controlling system for lean manufacturing [2]. The Kanban system is based on making visible what is otherwise intangible knowledge work, to ensure that the client's requests are delivered within the capacity of the system. Kanban uses a flow based delivery system through visual signals. This system is used to limit the quantity of work in progress.

Since last decade, Kanban have been adopted in software development and maintenance organizations [2], in order to apply flow based methodologies. From 2014 to 2015, the percentage of respondents who practiced Kanban techniques expanded from 31% to 39%. As Kanban popularity has increased, the number of people using work-in-progress and cycle time as measurements of agile success has grown as well [1].

© Springer International Publishing AG 2017
T. Silva da Silva et al. (Eds.): WBMA 2016, CCIS 680, pp. 110–121, 2017.
DOI: 10.1007/978-3-319-55907-0_10

However, the adoption of Kanban is not trivial [3]. The change of the team culture, already existing traditional development methods and conformity to prescriptive development models turn the dissemination of this practice more difficult. However, one of the crucial aspects is the lack of experience and the difficult training of new professionals in the use of Kanban. According to Ahmad et al. [3], the professional training is the major hurdle in adopting Kanban in organizations.

This article proposes SimKan, a technique that uses game elements (serious games) and stochastic simulation to reproduce simulation scenarios of software projects to train the use of Kanban. Simkan allow participants to experience in a short time and at low cost, the practice of the methodology. Its possible to collect metrics, accomplish discussions and gain experience without the risk and necessary time of a real project, with its characteristics and established commitments. SimKan is not based on software. Except for the metrics collection tasks, the entire job is done manually using paper, scotch tape, cards, and pen.

This paper is organized as follows: Sect. 2 describes the Kanban methodology, serious games and stochastic simulations. Section 3 presents SimKan, describing its concepts and steps to be followed. Section 4 presents the experiment and its results. Section 5 discusses the threats to the validity. Section 6 presents the related work and Sect. 7 concludes and points out possible future researches.

2   Background

To comprehend the functions of SimKan, it is necessary to know the main concepts related to Kanban, serious games and stochastic simulations. The following sections bring these themes to light.

2.1   Kanban

Kanban is a Japanese word and means "signal card" [4]. In manufacturing, kanban boards are used to inform at a certain stage of the production chain that the next step needs more production inputs and that these can already be produced. The responsible for a production stage can only work if a subsequent stage has activated him/her through a kanban. This series of stages in which the next one requests the work of the previous one, is what is called a "pull system": one stage requests or "pulls" the work of a previous one [5].

Kanban is a method that defines, manages and improves services that deliver knowledge work, such as professional services, creative efforts and the development of software products [2]. Some process management practices can be recommended for an implementation of this technique, like to visualize the workflow, to limit work in progress, to adjust and prioritize cadences, to measure the flow, to identify service classes, to establish service level agreements and to manage the workflow [6].

Besides the practice of process management, continuous improvement practices are adopted (e.g. inspection and adaptation), based on the principles of

Lean, deriving in more detailed actions and practice. To understand and apply these practices, it is necessary to comprehend some concepts which are contained in the literature about Kanban [2,4,6], whose definitions follow:

The development and maintenance of a software is usually based on a group of requests. There are various types of request, such as new functionality, changes in established features, fixing bugs. This group of work items comprises the **backlog**.

To work on the items of the backlog, passing them through the various phases of development or maintenance, it is necessary to create the **value chain** based on which the cycle is established. The value chain describes the phases through which an item has to pass to become a finished software. For example: backlog, requirements, analysis, project, implementation, tests, acceptance, and deployment.

Backlog items are probably not all of the same type, thus they will have different priorities. Probably there will be situations where the delivery of a functionality will be necessary at a certain date, or fixing a bug which has to be implemented immediately. Hence, the services need to be classified in **service classes** with their respective policies. An example could be: the definition of a service class of urgency called "expedition" by the stakeholder of the project and the establishment of a policy informing that this class will get priority treatment in all development process phases, including replacing tasks that are being executed.

Cadence is a concept in Kanban which determines the rhythm of a type of event. Priority, delivery, retrospectives and whichever recurring event can have its own cadence [4]. Although there are various activity types in a typical software development environment that can benefit from regular cadences, the most typical and the ones that need being considered are incoming and outcoming [6].

The Work in Progress - WIP is a set of work items which are in progress in the Kanban system. The reduction of the work in progress is associated by Anderson [4] to quality increase, deducing that it is necessary to invest in the management of the work in progress, introducing explicit rules to limiting it.

2.2   Stochastic Simulation

Simulation is the imitation of the operation of a real world system or process during a certain period of time [7]. Simulations are applied in various domains like Physics, Chemistry, Engineering and Economics with the aim to establish policies, perform tests with new equipments, verify hypothesis, perform professional training and others, thereby diminishing risks, costs and the time necessary used in a real process for these same activities. To perform a simulation, a functioning model of the system or the process to be studied is constructed.

Simulation models can be deterministic or stochastic. When they are deterministic there are no random variable factors involved, and with a given entry value, the return value of the model will always be the same. With random variables the model is called stochastic, and as a consequence, random entries will lead to random return values and the operated measures have to be taken as statistics of real return values of the system or of the process [7].

2.3 Serious Games

Serious games are games that explore concepts or simulates real situations with purpose to accomplish a task, such as aircraft piloting or medical surgeries. Its primary purpose is not to entertain, but to use playful elements to stimulate engagement to the task [8].

According to Abt [9] serious games deliver "dramatic representations" of the subject or problem which is studied and permit the players to assume realistic roles, face problems, elaborate strategies, take decisions and get a fast feedback about the consequences of their actions, without the costs of the consequences or mistakes in the real world.

3   The SimKan Approach

SimKan is an approach which proposes a simulation of the use of Kanban for activities in the maintenance of a software system which is already in use. It consists of a serious game and is elaborated in a stochastic way, using a normal dice casting with six sides to introduce randomness in points like finishing of an activity or the entry of a certain type of activity into the system. Using these concepts the participants are able to experience the main practices of Kanban, training thus the use of the method in real projects, without the necessity to await the conventional cycle of a project to observe the utilization forms and results of Kanban.

During a section of SimKan, a backlog with m items is taken, being n of them of the service class "expedition" and the others of standard service class. For the last one, the items are distributed in sets of k with high priority, k with average priority and p $(p = k + 4)$ with low priority. The decision to execute the simulation with more low priority items was taken, adding four more items in this category, but these values may be adjusted in various executions. The following exercises were proposed: visualization of work flow through the use of a kanban board, experimentation of limits for work in progress, adjustment tests in the income cadence, use of service classes, and measurement and generation of flow graphics.

3.1 Execution Parameters

The work items are distributed in two service classes: "standard" applicable to all items and "expedition" for items that need to be immediately treated, like bugs in productive environments. For the standard class the established policy is, once selected by the team for service within the work in progress limits, its items have to be attended to according to their priority: high, average or low respectively. For the "expedition" class the overriding of imposed limits is permitted for the quantity of work in progress, although there will be only one item of this type in the Kanban system and it will be treated with priority over all other items.

Being an approach based on stochastic simulations [7] SimKan uses the conventional throw of dice with six sides as definition what would be considered as a finished activity. To determine what is considered a working day, the following rule was adopted: all team participants threw the dice. After the last team member threw the dice the period was considered as a finished working day.

To simulate priority meetings a raffle of the backlog items was adopted, including only those not in the expedition class. To simulate the entry of items of the expedition class into the system, the casting of dice was also used in a certain point of the flowchart, like showed in Fig. 1.

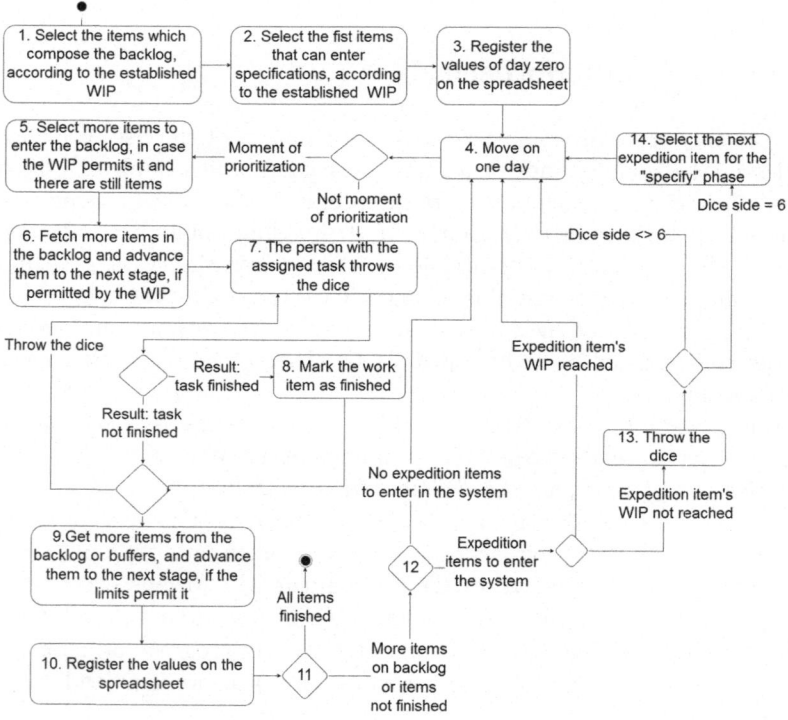

Fig. 1. Experiment execution flow

To minimize a possible discussion about the initial value chain and limits to the work in progress to be adopted in the beginning, the chain showed in Fig. 2 is established with its respective limits (showed between parenthesis next to the title of each stage) and separated by rays (horizontal lines) for the items of "standard" and "expedition" classes, respectively. Continuing the established

	Backlog (5)	Specification (2)	Development (2)	Integrated Tests (1)	Ready to Deploy
Standard Class					
Expedition Class (WIP = 1)					

Fig. 2. Value chain 1

politics for service classes, the expedition class allows only one item at a time and therefore there is the note "(WIP=1)".

3.2   Preparation

The team needs to distribute their roles which are: specifiers, implementers and testers. In a five-people team for example there would be two specifiers, two implementers and one tester.

It is important to highlight that the only component that is not manual is the electronic spreadsheet to collect the metrics and to plot the graphics. All others, such as the Kanban board and the work item cards, are made manually on paper, with scotch tape, cards and pens.

After the definition of the roles, the initial value chain has to be established on a wall (or on a table) and the items of the backlog written on post it cards. The items of the "expedition" class are written on post its with a different colour than those of the "standard" class.

3.3   Execution Flow

Figure 1 shows the flowchart of SimKan, whose steps are detailed as following:

1. Select the items which compose the backlog, according to the established WIP: The team selects the items of the standard class among the existing maintenance backlog to start the service. This choice obeys the limit of WIP (5 items at the beginning of the experiment) established in the value chain.
2. Select the first items that can enter specifications, according to the established WIP. The specifiers choose the first items to be attended to among the selected backlog.
3. Register the values of day zero on the spreadsheet: One of the participants writes the current situation of the system on the metrics spreadsheet.
4. Move on one day. After all the team members throw the dice, a working day ends.
5. Select more items to enter the backlog, in case the WIP permits it and there are still items; this step simulates the incoming cadence of the working items into the system. A moment of prioritization happens every fifth workday and, attending to the established limits for the quantity of permitted items to the backlog column, new working items are selected to enter the system.
6. Fetch more items in the backlog and advance them to the next stage, if permitted by the WIP. The responsible component for specification, respecting the limits of work in progress, pulls one or more items of the column "backlog" to the column "specification".

7. The person with the assigned task throws the dice: each team component responsible for a work item throws the dice. If the result is odd, the item is concluded. If not, nothing happens and the next team component throws the dice, until everyone threw the dice.

8. Mark the work item as finished: if the casting executed in step 7 resulted in an odd number, the person who threw the dice has his task finished and will register this conclusion on the board. It is possible to do that in placing his card in the column of the chart that indicates the finished item, if such a column exists, or marking something on the working item card to inform that it was concluded.

9. Get more items from the backlog or buffers, and advance them to the next stage, if the limits permit it: after the casting of the dice by all team members, the moment arrives to "pull" items to the next stage of the value chain. Respecting the established limits of the work in progress, the team advances the work item cards which are ready for the next stage.

10. Register the values on the spreadsheet: one of the team components registers the current situation of the Kanban system on the metrics spreadsheet.

11. If there are still work items: the process continues until all work items are finished. When this happens, the simulation is considered ended.

12. The entry of items of the "expedition" class into the system: after the elapse of a working day and if the limit of permitted items in the system for the "expedition" class has not been attained, a random entry of an item of this class is simulated through the casting of the dice. One of the participants throws the dice (step 13) and if the number 6 is drawn, the item enters the system and is selected for the column "specification" (step 14).

4   Assessment of SimKan

A controlled approach execution was carried out to assess SimKan with the aim to answer the following research question:

RQ1: SimKan facilitates the knowledge dissemination about Kanban and its practices?

To answer the RQ1 research question an experiment was carried out following the flow and rules mentioned in Sect. 3.3.

4.1   Participants

The experiment was executed with a team of 5 persons. All participants are graduated in Computer Science or Electric Engineering. Four of them have a master degree and were selected because of their large experience in software development. Two participants have been acting for some years as project leaders, conducting during most of the time, software maintenance projects. The other ones are experienced in the exercise of roles such as developers, requirements analysts, configuration managers, testers and software architects.

4.2 Execution

Once the participants were selected, the board set and the items described on post it cards, the team started the flow execution with the raffle of the first five items for the backlog, obeying the established limit of work in progress, afterwards executing the following steps. There was a period of adaptation to the execution process and on the third "day" (the time of the simulation used in the game, represented by rounds of casting), there was a discussion in the team about who would be the next person to pick up an activity to execute, due to the conclusion of some activities of the initial stages. Based on this discussion, the team felt the need to execute the first adjustment, to put "ready" columns for the "specification" and "implementation" stages. Thereby the value chain was set up on the board, showing now the following phases and their respective limits for WIP: Backlog (5), Specification (2), Specification Done (2), Implementation (2) Implementation Done (2), Integrated Tests (1), Ready to Deploy.

Despite this first fit, the team noticed moments of idleness of some participants. The execution continued, and on the twelfth "day" there was a new fit in the value chain, as shown in Fig. 3.

	5	4		4		1	
	Backlog	Specification	Specification Done	Development	Development Done	Integrated Tests	Ready to Deploy
Standard Class							
Expedition Class (WIP = 1)							

Fig. 3. Value chain 3

For "Specification" the limit of four activities in progress was adopted, considering within this limit the activities being in the stage "Specification Done". For "Implementation" the limit was also four activities, with the same consideration for the stage "Implementation Done". After this adjustment the idleness of some components remained. This fact and the perception of the bottleneck in test activities, lead to new adjustment on the seventeenth "day", considering the role adjustment in the team and the establishment of new limits of work in progress. Until this moment every person was specialized in one role. From this "day" on, the implementers would also act as testers and the limit for integrated tests was established in two.

After this last adjustment, the execution continued until the conclusion of all 25 work items, totalizing 39 execution "days". It is important to report that the three items of the expedition class were attended to during the execution of the experiment with their system entry according to the random criteria defined in the flowchart.

4.3 Data Collection

During the experiment the data collection was made about the progress of the activities. Figure 4 shows the cumulative flow diagram of the system. It is possible

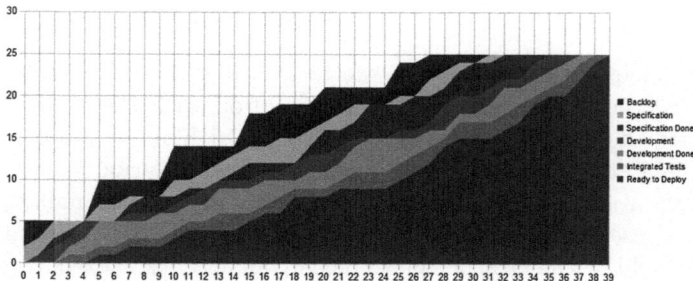

Fig. 4. Cumulative flow diagram

to notice that there was no continuous activity flow between the stages in the value chain, mainly on the first days.

It could be observed for example that on the second "day" there was no item in the backlog. That could be interpreted as an indication that the limit of 5 items should be increased. On the eighth "day" despite of having an item in the backlog, there was no activity in "specification" going on. In this case it was possible to verify an idleness because the limit for work in progress for the next stage had already been attained, preventing the prosecution in the activity flow.

On the first days of the experiment, the lead time increased, but as the time passed, it became a trend, which enabled us to establish an inferior and superior limit. With these limits it was possible to define service level agreements, for example, that 90% of the work would be finished in 16 "days". The lead times for items of the expedition class were, 7, 9 and 8 days respectively, in an average of 8 days.

Another piece of information obtained as a result of the experiment was the variation of team component's idleness over the time. Though it is not a common Kanban metric, it showed to be important for the team to guide some of the decision making. Such an example would be when the implementers started to act as testers too, decision taken based on the analysis of idleness and bottlenecks existing in the "integrated tests".

4.4   Discussion

Although a fast theoretical explanation of the Kanban Principles was given to the experiment participants, **the necessary time for it was short, not longer than an hour**. On the other hand, it's believed that the presence of an experienced facilitator to support the execution of the simulation is necessary for a positive realization of a SimKan training session.

To answer the proposed RQ1 research question, an assessment questionnaire was prepared, which was answered by the participants, containing the following questions:

1. Which was your prior Kanban knowledge and practice before participation on the simulation?

2. The realization of the simulation permitted you to amplify our knowledge about Kanban and its practice?
3. After the simulation, what perception do you have about your knowledge level in Kanban practice?

As a result of the first question 20% of the participants answered, that they had no previous knowledge of Kanban what so ever. For the other 80% the previous knowledge was classified as "low". The second question: 20% agreed partially that the approach enabled them to acquire Kanban knowledge and its practice and the other 80% agreed totally. The third question asked the participants to classify their perception of their knowledge level about Kanban after the realization on SimKan, with the options "no", "low", "intermediate" and "high", to which 60% answered "intermediate" and 40% "high".

During the evaluation session, the interest and commitment of the participants in the execution of the simulation was observed. They considered the form of the simulation as "playful" and interesting, rising discussions about idleness, work progress, information collecting and about the technique of Kanban in itself, which would take an enormous amount of time in conventional cycles in a software project. The participants in the experiment, although experienced in software development, had never experienced Kanban and its practices, and the experiment enabled them to acquire these techniques in a playful way.

The employed technique contributes to a fast training of teams who intend to start to migrate to Kanban, reducing the necessary time for training and permitting situation simulations of a real project. Furthermore in many organizations, the training realization needs some level of formality and bureaucracy, tending to consume more time to acquire the knowledge. The hereby suggested simulation does not need major formality, laboratories and complicated tools, only few material, an electronic spreadsheet and a facilitator who supports the execution, **which permits a faster disruption of lethargy/inertia of comprehension of Kanban in new teams**.

5 Threats to Validity

The main threat to validity concerns the fact, that the proposal was not executed many times. It is necessary to do this to attain a better based conclusion in relation to the results.

6 Related Studies

As Kanban has its origin in the area of manufacturing, the simulation of its use in this kind of processes is easy to find. Kochel and Nielander [10] describe a simulator to treat the optimization of multi stages Kanban systems. Hao and Shen [11] proposed a simulation model for complex processes of material manipulations, based on a kanban system.

In software development some researches that propose simulations of agile maintenance processes can be listed. Lunesu [12] proposes a model of software process simulation for Lean and Kanban and has conducted the construction of a software simulation based on events. Anderson et al. [13] also propose a simulation process to establish a comparison between Scrum and Kanban. These research differ from the current proposed research form, as the simulation in this research counts with the participation of persons and uses a dice to introduce stochastic characteristics in the process, and the above mentioned were executed through a software, which, depending on the implemented mechanism, tends to inhibit discussions and learning of the method.

Other types of related studies are about games to teach Kanban. Heikkila et al. [14] presents a collaborative game to teach Kanban at a university. Called GetKanban, it differs from this research in being a board game and not a simulation.

7   Conclusion and Future Research

Professional training in software processes almost never is trivial and the normally theoretical or not very practical character of traditional training leaves gaps of knowledge and few real situation learning. Traditional learning can be boring, or it can not achieve a necessary engagement level in the students. This paper proposes SimKan, an approach to train teams for using Kanban, which is based on the execution of a serious game, using stochastic simulation on a Kanban system.

Simkan uses an execution flow which enables learning the main practice of Kanban, using a backlog of functionalities and showing its evolution through the value chain, using the casting of a dice of six sides as a parameter to simulate specific issues of execution, like finished task or entry of an item of higher priority into the system.

To verify the functioning of SimKan an experiment was realized using the approach in a team without experience on Kanban and through a specific questionnaire, to collect the perception of learning knowledge of Kanban after SimKan usage.

According to the applied assessment questionnaire, 80% agreed totally that SimKan permits to acquire knowledge about Kanban practices. After the execution of SimKan the level of Kanban was classified as "intermediate" by 60% of the participants and "high" by 40%. Thus it can be concluded that SimKan is adequate to train teams in Kanban, bringing positive results in a short time and at low cost, in a playful training process which generates engagement.

A future research deriving from this study, could be the realization of an experiment using a greater number of interactions. Moreover the implementation of new studies about the adaptations which occur during the simulation, considering the fact that Kanban is an evolutionary approach and simulation techniques will be used to contemplate this aspect. Some questions about the fit which occurred during the game continue unanswered. The adaptations continued? Which of them were relevant to the Kanban reality and which were a result of the simulation? Is there a necessity to fix an initial value chain?

Despite the fact of SimKam uses only manual tools, there are no constraints for its implementation through a software, which could also be listed as a possible future research.

Another point of a future research comes from the observation of the simulation execution. A high level of engagement of the participants was noticed because the team needed to be totally focused and this reduced the level of distraction. A comparative study focusing on the traditional training - where the students observe and the teacher exposes - and on the study of the effectiveness of SimKan to obtain more focus and to improve real learning, is necessary.

References

1. VersionOne: 10th annual state of agile report (2015). http://stateofagile. versionone.com/
2. Anderson, D., Carmichael, A.: Essential Kanban Condensed. Lean Kanban University Press (2016)
3. Ahmad, M.O., Markkula, J., Oivo, M.: Kanban in software development: a systematic literature review. In: 2013 39th Euromicro Conference on Software Engineering and Advanced Applications, pp. 9–16. IEEE (2013)
4. Anderson, D.J.: Kanban: Mudanca Evolucionaria de Sucesso Para Seu Negocio de Tecnologia. Blue Hole Press (2011)
5. Poppendieck, M., Poppendieck, T.: Lean Software Development: An Agile Toolkit: An Agile Toolkit. Addison-Wesley, Boston (2003)
6. Boeg, J.: Kanban em 10 passos. Tradução de Leonardo Campos, Marcelo Costa, Lúcio Camilo, Rafael Buzon, Paulo Rebelo, Eric Fer, Ivo La Puma, Leonardo Galvão, Thiago Vespa, Manoel Pimentel e Daniel Wildt. C4Media (2010)
7. Santos, M.P.: Introdução à simulação discreta. UERJ, Rio de Janeiro (1999)
8. Michael, D.R., Chen, S.L.: Serious games. Games that educate, train, and inform (lernmaterialien): Games that educate, train, and info (2005)
9. Abt, C.C.: Serious Games. University Press of America, Lanham (1987)
10. Köchel, P., Nieländer, U.: Kanban optimization by simulation and evolution. Prod. Planning Control 13(8), 725–734 (2002)
11. Hao, Q., Shen, W.: Implementing a hybrid simulation model for a kanban-based material handling system. Rob. Comput. Integr. Manuf. 24(5), 635–646 (2008)
12. Lunesu, M.I.: Process software simulation model of lean-kanban approach (2013)
13. Anderson, D.J., Concas, G., Lunesu, M.I., Marchesi, M., Zhang, H.: A comparative study of scrum and kanban approaches on a real case study using simulation. In: Wohlin, C. (ed.) XP 2012. LNBIP, vol. 111, pp. 123–137. Springer, Heidelberg (2012). doi:10.1007/978-3-642-30350-0_9
14. Heikkilä, V.T., Paasivaara, M., Lassenius, C.: Teaching university students kanban with a collaborative board game. In: Proceedings of the 38th International Conference on Software Engineering Companion, pp. 471–480. ACM (2016)

Short Papers

Predicting the Unpredictable: Using Monte Carlo Simulation to Predict Project Completion Date

Lucas Colucci$^{(\boxtimes)}$ and Raphael Albino

Plataformatec, São Paulo, SP, Brazil
{lucas.colucci,raphael.albino}@plataformatec.com.br

Abstract. If you work with software development you will probably face two important, but not always convergent, aspects: scope and delivery cadence. The process of aligning the expectations of product increment and team throughput is usually arduous but, when this happens, it improves the chances of project success. Stakeholders frequently want the project done faster than it is possible for us to do it. And then, when they ask the date on which we will finish the work, we never have the right answer. In the last two years, while working with different projects at Plataformatec, we have been trying to solve that problem in many different ways: mean throughput, linear regression and even manually adjusting our predictions. However, all of them had their drawbacks. This paper presents what we think will be the best approach to forecast project deadline: Monte Carlo Simulation. We explain how it works, how to apply it in a project and how you can benefit from using it.

Keywords: Monte carlo simulation · Statistics · Project management · Metrics · Agile methodology · Prediction · Forecast

1 Introduction

Deadline is a delicate subject in software development project regardless of the technique used e.g. traditional, agile etc. The stakeholders always think the date is too far away and, on the other hand, team members believe they do not have enough time to finish what was agreed on.

Using Agile Software Development (ASD), software is developed incrementally in small iterations, and customer feedback serves as an important input for subsequent iterations. This also implies that estimations and plans need to be done progressively [4].

In an effort to support the alignment between business and technology, agile metrics are widespread inside agile companies in order to monitor work and tend to make improvements inside them [3].

To understand how much work is being delivered, we usually measure throughput as the number of work items (e.g. user story) that a team finishes in

© Springer International Publishing AG 2017
T. Silva da Silva et al. (Eds.): WBMA 2016, CCIS 680, pp. 125–130, 2017.
DOI: 10.1007/978-3-319-55907-0_11

a week. This metric helps us in having deadline predictability. It is also useful to identify problems that could be occurring in the software development process.

During the past two years, while trying to predict projects' completion date, we had used three different approaches. After some research, we found out a new technique: Monte Carlo Simulation; and it seems to be what we were looking for.

In this paper, we present the methodologies that we tried to use before, and explain why they did not please us. Later we present the current solution and expatiate on why we think it could be a better method as well as the pros and cons of using it.

2   Methodologies Background

We have been testing prediction methods for a long time, and all of them had some drawbacks, which could not be ignored. The methods that we used were: mean throughput, linear regression and a throughput percentile approach.

2.1   Mean Throughput

A common concern about using throughput to predict delivery dates is the requirement of relatively similar story sizes in the backlog. If not followed, the large standard deviation could affect directly the predictions, which directly affects the use of average to predict deadlines.

Mean throughput is the easiest approach that one could possibly think of. It works by simply calculating the project's average throughput based on its past data. However, projects will rarely have a distribution in which average, median, and mode are similar. Therefore, as data becomes skewed, the average loses its ability to provide the best central location.

2.2   Linear Regression

Linear regression is a common next step for data-driven teams. Thus we followed the same path. We started using it to predict when the regression line would reach the backlog size in our burn-up chart.

It seemed to be working fine back then, but we reached two main problems with that approach:

- We considered that the backlog would not change with time. Which is biased, since in all of our projects the backlog indeed changed;
- When we use Linear Regression, we are making some assumptions. One of them is multivariate normality. The linear regression analysis requires all variables to be multivariate normal [1]. When we put all our throughput data into a statistical analysis, we saw that it did not fit into a normal distribution.

Since we did not know a methodology that would bind the prediction of the backlog and throughput growth, we have decided to focus on the second problem and start using an ad hoc approach.

2.3   Manual Setting

In our methodology, we studied the percentiles of our throughput history. For example, we would analyze what was the throughput 95%, 80% and 50% of the weeks. With that in mind, we could manually add three different projections, one for each percentile. The result would be a range of dates in which the project could be completed. We considered a higher percentile analysis more pessimistic and a lower one more optimistic. But the static backlog problem was not solved and, therefore, made us take a step further and try a new approach.

3   Monte Carlo Simulation

Monte Carlo simulation is a type of simulation that relies on repeated random sampling and statistical analysis to compute the results. This method of simulation is very closely related to random experiments, for which the specific result is not known in advance [2].

Monte Carlo techniques have started to appear in commercial software development project management tools, with an emphasis on modelling the uncertainty of work estimate size. These tools help account for variability surrounding team velocity and work estimate [5].

Next, we will present a simple example and then show how we used it in real world.

3.1   Dice Game

Imagine you are playing a dice game in which the goal is to reach a sum of 12 points, with the least number of rolls. The best play here would be 2 consecutive rolls in which you get a 6 in each of them, and the worst would be 12 rolls getting a 1. What we want to calculate is the probability of ending the game after N runs.

We consider that we are rolling a 6-face dice, thus we have 6 possible outcomes for each roll. The probability of reaching the 12 point threshold in the first roll is zero, since the maximum value on the dice is 6.

On the second roll, to win you would need two consecutive 6:

$$P(x) = \frac{1}{6} * \frac{1}{6} \approx 2.78\% \tag{1}$$

In the third roll you can achieve 12 points in many ways: (3, 3, 6), (5, 5, 2), (4, 4, 4), etc. The probability is not as easy anymore. That is when Monte Carlo Simulation (MCS) comes handy.

What MCS does is to simulate thousands of dice rolls and then analyze the outcome. For example, to know the probability of finishing the game on the third round, it would roll the dice three times, sum the points and store that result. After that, it would repeat those steps N times (where N is usually greater than 1000) and summarize how many rolls each sum of points got.

Now, what we do is to sum all the occurrences that generated a sum greater than 12 and divide it by the total. In this case, we ran it and the result, with N = 5000 was 37%. The same way we did it for the third round, we could do it for the fourth, fifth, and so on.

3.2   Real World

The real world solution is very similar to the dice rolling example. The only difference is that we vary the goal as well (the 12 points in the game scenario), to consider the change in the backlog.

So now, the possible outcome for each round is our throughput history. And, in the same way we are "rolling dices" for our throughput, we need do the same for our backlog in order to give it the chance to grow as well. In this case the possible outcomes would be the Backlog Growth Rate (BGR).

We define BGR of the week x as:

$$BGR(x) = \begin{cases} backlogSize(x) - backlogSize(x-1), & \text{if } x \geq 2 \\ 0, & \text{otherwise} \end{cases} \quad (2)$$

Let's say our project's current state is as presented on Table 1.

Table 1. Project current state.

Week number	Throughput history	Backlog history
1	2	15 stories (BGR 0)
2	3	17 stories (BGR 2)
3	0	18 stories (BGR 1)
4	2	19 stories (BGR 1)
5	5	21 stories (BGR 2)
6	0	22 stories (BGR 1)
7	1	22 stories (BGR 0)
8	3	24 stories (BGR 2)
9	3	24 stories (BGR 0)

Our possible plays in each round, for the throughput, would be the set {2, 3, 0, 2, 5, 0, 1, 3, 3} and for the BGR would be {0, 2, 1, 1, 2, 1, 0, 2, 0}. We do not exclude repeated numbers because, with them, we can maintain the higher probability of having a number instead of others.

Now, we can apply here the same rationale behind the dice game. Some of the possible outcomes for the first round are illustrated in Table 2.

Then, we would run many like those and see how many have a throughput sum greater than the backlog sum, and then divide the result by the number of runs. Doing that, we would have the probability of completing the project in

Table 2. Part of sample project Monte Carlo simulation first round.

Throughput "Roll"	BGR "Roll"	Throughput sum	Backlog sum
2	0	$18+2 = 20$	$24+0 = 24$
2	2	$18+2 = 20$	$24+2 = 26$
2	1	$18+2 = 20$	$24+1 = 25$
3	0	$18+3 = 21$	$24+0 = 24$
3	2	$18+3 = 21$	$24+2 = 26$
3	1	$18+3 = 21$	$24+1 = 25$
0	0	$18+0 = 18$	$24+0 = 24$
0	2	$18+0 = 18$	$24+2 = 26$

the first week. For the next week we would do the same, but then rolling the dice twice in each round and summing them for both the throughput and the backlog.

A problem that this method has is that the backlog at the beginning of a project behaves differently than at the middle or end of it, due to different contexts.

To solve this problem, instead of considering the whole BGR history as the possible outcomes, we consider only the last 10 BGRs from the backlog, which would give us a more accurate context. We can tune the number of BGRs according to each project, but 10 worked fine for most of our data.

The result for the next 10 weeks, using the new last-ten-BGR approach, is represented in Fig. 1.

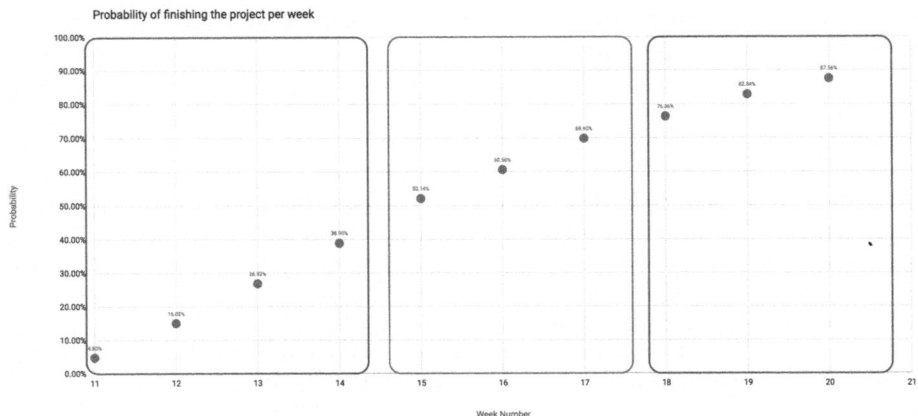

Fig. 1. Monte Carlo simulation over our project's data.

As you can see, we highlighted three different areas on the chart to illustrate what we think could be considered takeaways:

- The first area groups the weeks in which we have less than 50% probability of finishing the project. For us, it means it would be too risky to tell your project's stakeholders that you would finish in those weeks.
- The next area illustrates the weeks in which we have a probability between 50% and 75% of finishing the project. If the stakeholders are pressuring you to deliver fast, those are the weeks that, if you take a leap of faith and improve your process, you may be able finish.
- The last is a more risk-free area, where you have a probability greater than 75% of completing the project by those weeks. We suggest that you always give preference to estimate the end of your project based on this area, but we know we cannot always be that safe.

We tested the MCS in past projects and it seems to work really well, but, as in any other statistical method, it gets much better after some weeks into the project than at the beginning.

4   Summary

Tracking throughput means that the team is looking for process improvements based on numbers, which could make the process more transparent for all stakeholders, but it is important to take care when using the method.

Predicting when a project is likely to end seems too "hokus-pokus" and Monte Carlo simulation is really easy to implement and gives a much better prediction and understanding of our project. It is important to make it clear that this method is a statistical method, thus it is not fail proof. The main goal is to add an element to your toolkit and make project management easier. We, at Plataformatec, do not only rely on Monte Carlo Simulation to define deadlines and predict project deliveries. It is just an extra piece to make more rational decisions.

References

1. Osborne, J.W., Waters, E.: Four assumptions of multiple regression that researchers should always test. Pract. Assess. Res. Eval. **8**, 1–5 (2002)
2. Raychaudhuri, S.: Introduction to Monte Carlo simulation. In: Proceedings of the 2008 Winter Simulation Conference, pp. 91–100 (2008)
3. Brezonik, L., Majer, C.: Grid information services for distributed resource sharing. In: Proceedings of the SQAMIA 2016: 5th Workshop of Software Quality, Analysis, Monitoring, Improvement, and Applications, Budapest, Hungary (2016)
4. Usman, M., Mendes, E., Weidt, F., Britto, R.: Effort estimation in agile software development: a systematic literature review. In: Proceedings of the 10th International Conference on Predictive Models in Software Engineering, Turin, Italy (2014)
5. Magennis, T.: Managing software development risk using modeling and monte carlo simulation. In: Proceedings of the Lean Software and Systems Consortium 2012 Conference in Boston, Massachusetts, USA (2012)

Scrum Hero: Gamifying the Scrum Framework

Jamila Peripolli Souza$^{(\boxtimes)}$, André Ricardo Zavan, and Daniela Eloise Flôr

Graduate Program in Technology in Systems Analysis and Development,
Instituto Federal do Paraná (IFPR), Campus Paranavaí, Paranavaí, PR, Brazil
milaperipolli@outlook.com,
{andre.zavan,daniela.flor}@ifpr.edu.br

Abstract. This short paper presents a framework proposal for the planning and the management of software projects based on Scrum, using gamification techniques. The objective of the proposal is to verify how the gamification can interfere in the motivation and efficiency of a team in a real development environment.

Keywords: Gamification · Scrum · Software engineering · Agile

1 Introduction

In analyzing the current scenario of software development, it is possible to realize that, in spite of all the efforts of software engineering, many projects show problems in this area. As said Standish Group in CHAOS Report [1], only 29% of the software projects are successfully completed.

One of the challenges faced by the development companies is to maintain a team working hard on a project, because this is an activity that requires great mental strength. This can be pointed out as one of the main causes of failures in IT projects (Information Technology), which according to a research carried out by Geneca [2], 75% of the project members do not expect the project to be successful. Furthermore, Feath [3] shows that many IT projects fail due to a lack of focus from its team members.

It is believed that a possible solution to increase the efforts and motivation of the developers would be to insert gamification within the development environment. As described by Junior [4], gamification can involve people and make their activities funnier, and also motivating the developers to complete their work.

2 Objective

The objective is to adapt the Scrum framework to the project's planning and monitoring by using gamification techniques. We also intend to evaluate the real effects of using custom framework and test it on a real software development environment and applying the parameters of on-time releases, customer satisfaction and, mainly, team motivation.

In order to achieve the general goal of this research, the following specific goals were defined:

T. Silva da Silva et al. (Eds.): WBMA 2016, CCIS 680, pp. 131–135, 2017.
DOI: 10.1007/978-3-319-55907-0_12

- Study the gamification and the Scrum framework in order to find games' elements, which can be used during the software development and find where to put them in the Scrum;
- Adapt the Scrum framework in order to integrate it with the gamification by incorporating elements such as score, achievements, levels and experience (XP) to the artifacts, ceremonies and Scrum's roles;
- To deploy and to evaluate the use of a gamified framework in a real environment of software production;
- To analyze and to describe the results obtained by the use of gamification applied to Scrum, comparing them with historical data from the development company.

3   Methodology

The research began with a bibliographic survey of the following themes: agile methodologies, Scrum, gamification and related areas. Within them, we looked for ways to insert gamification into the process of the Scrum framework.

Then, Scrum was mapped as a game, having a main challenge (the project under development), secondary challenges (the ceremonies), tertiary challenges (daily tasks), as well as challenges concurrent to the progress of the game (professional improvement). Besides, we also added rewards and levels. The mapping was done based on RPG games (Role Playing Game), due to its purpose of a continuous narrative and the characters' evolution.

In order to evaluate the results, the custom framework was tested in a real development environment, where the data management was carried out with aid from a software prototype (Scrum Hero Manager) and questions to collect information. Then, all this data will be compared with the historical data, which had already been collected by the company, using the same format as the quiz, thus making it possible to verify how the gamification use may affect the team motivation, their on-time releases and the customer satisfaction.

4   Theoretical Base

According to Schwaber [5], Scrum is an interactive and incremental framework that focus on frequent releases, adding the highest business values to the customer in the shortest time possible. Its structure is based on job cycles called Sprints, where one or more features are developed by the team in each Sprint and then added to the software after the validation made by the PO (Product Owner). In addition to validate the increment, the PO is also responsible for maintaining the necessary requirements to complete the product development. The Scrum also benefits from the Scrum Master, which is responsible for ensuring that the team has conditions to work in a productive way, removing any impediments.

In contrast to this, the gamification consists in bringing game elements to a real life context. As pointed out by Junior [4], with instantaneous rewards, a feeling of progression, constant positive feedback and challenges, human beings generate dopamine e serotonin, both enzymes that generate a pleasure sensation in our brains, which in its turn directs the participants' behavior by rewarding them with the pleasure of the joy.

The present study integrates gamification elements into Scrum, aiming at maintaining the positive aspects there is in both concepts.

5   Scrum Hero

The customized framework is called Scrum Hero, and it follows the same structure as Scrum, including its roles, ceremonies and artifacts. Furthermore, it also adds playful elements such as game terms, scores, characters, rankings, challenges, rewards, medals, and trophies.

In Scrum Hero, the customers are treated like mystical entities that interfere in the Clan's life (the Scrum team). The PO is the Product Oracle, which keeps the Warriors (the development team) up-to-date with the mystical entities desires, and, then, the Scrum Master becomes the Scrum Healer, who is responsible for helping the Clan in all the challenges and conflicts, and for expelling the Stone Monsters (impediments) during the Quests (Sprints).

Each player can have their individual Skills, that is a specific ability related to technology, and in each game (project) the company needs to define which skills they are going to apply. The Skill score makes it possible to know which players have more affinity with a certain Skill, which is useful to allocate professionals in a teamwork, since the Skill score indicates the individual Skills of each person.

There are three kinds of scores in Scrum Hero. Each player has their own scores, but there is no score for the Clan. The easiest scores to achieve are the Score Points (PT), which are obtained when the player concludes their daily tasks. This kind of score has a short duration; at the end of each project, it is reset. The most difficult scores to achieve are the Experience Points (XP), which are acquired when the players fulfill their achievements. This kind of score has a long duration, it continues valid until the end of the current project. Finally, there is another kind of score with a long duration, named the Skill Points (SP). The Skills of each player have their own scores, which are achieved upon completing a task, which requires this particular Skill.

Scrum Hero also brings other kinds of rewards, as follows:

- Medals - Related to Skills, each Skill can also be awarded a bronze, silver, or a gold medal.
- Trophies - Related to achievements, each achievement completed within the project can be awarded a bronze, silver, or gold trophy.
- Real rewards - They are defined by the company and can be achieved at the end of the Quests, as well as at the end of the game.

As the players gain experience, scores, and rewards, they can increase their level. The following levels, in ascending order of difficulty: Newbie, Guardian, Knight, Ninja, and Hero.

In addition to mapping the roles and ceremonies in Scrum, the artifacts are also mapped in Scrum Hero in order to deal with all the Scrum elements as if they belong to a game, thereby stimulating the game spirit of the players. The Scrum Hero artifacts are:

- Wish list (Product backlog) - The wish lists of the Mystical entities;
- Task list (Sprint backlog) - The task lists of the Quests;
- Burn down maps (Burn down charts) - Maps of the Quests and of the game;
- Offering (Increment) - Offerings made during the Quests to please the Mystical entities;
- Offering accepted (Increment validated by the Product oracle) - Offerings which were accepted by the Mystical entities;

The Scrum Sprints were mapped in Scrum Hero as the Quests; each Quest has a goal and tasks that must be performed by the Warriors. As well as the Scrum, the Quests begin after a planning meeting (Quest Planning); on each day of the Quest, there is a daily meeting (Daily Challenge), and at the end of every Quest there are two meetings, the Quest Challenge and the Clan Improvement meetings.

During each ceremony held in Scrum Hero, there are small challenges which can generate rewards for the players. Each time a player participates in or finishes an expected goal, they will receive some kind of reward. The possible rewards, participations and the Scrum Hero dynamic itself are illustrated in Fig. 1, below.

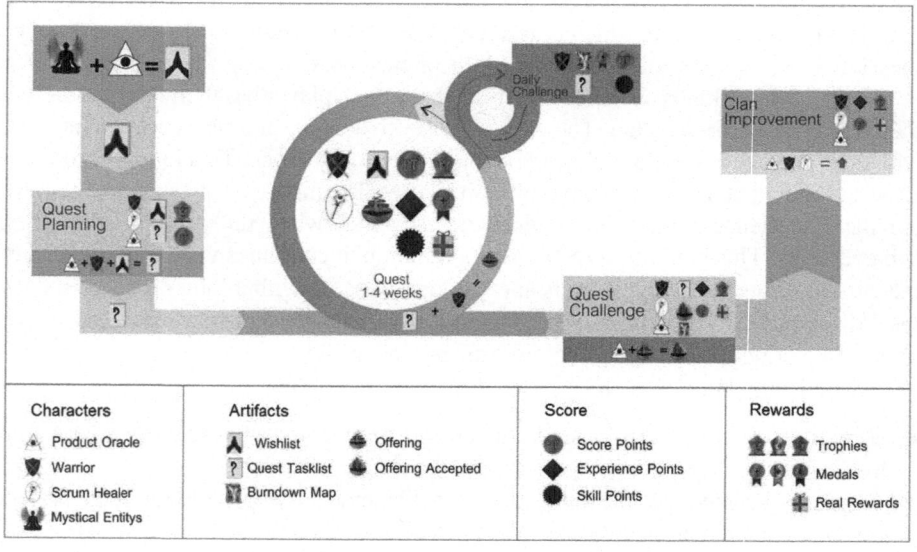

Fig. 1. Scrum Hero's operational structure.

6   Scrum Hero Manager

As the objective of facilitating the control of the Wishlist, Tasklists, scores, Skills and rewards, we developed a software prototype named Scrum Hero Manager. It helps in managing of the gamification techniques and the data, which will be used to analyze the results of this study.

The Scrum Hero Manager allows the management of players, Wishes, Tasks, Real Rewards, Achievements, Quests and Skills, besides the automatic scores assignments as the players complete their tasks.

7   Preliminary Results and Future Studies

During the test phase of Scrum Hero, four Quests were realized by teams consisting of four people each, being one Product Oracle, one Scrum Healer and two Warriors. The releases were made on time in 75% of the Quests. This result shows an astonishing increase by 55% compared to historical data from the company. The next step in the evaluation of the results will be to apply the quizzes about the customer satisfaction and the team motivation. In sequence, we will compare them to the historical data, permitting us to evaluate the real effects of using the Scrum Hero.

By applying the Scrum Hero in a real development environment, it was possible to observe some difficulties that can be facilitated in future studies. Therefore, in addition to concluding this research, the following suggestions for future studies are:

- Conclude the development of the Scrum Hero Manager;
- Improve the game mapping made inside the Scrum framework;
- Apply the Scrum Hero in an environment, which can encourage the game spirit of the players, for example, maintaining a ranking visible to all players all the time;
- Allow new Clan members to be added, making it possible to measure and assign XP and SP to each player according to their individual professional experiences;
- Add TDD (Test Driven Development) techniques or other techniques that aim at the quality of the code produced, ensuring that the urgency in completing the tasks will not compromise the quality of the work;
- Develop an adaptation of the Scrum Hero focused on the teaching and learning areas.

References

1. Standish Group: CHAOS report (2015). http://blog.standishgroup.com/post/50
2. Geneca: Up to 75% of business and IT executives anticipate their software projects will fail, Oak Brook (2011). http://www.geneca.com/75-business-executives-anticipate-software-projects-fail/
3. Feath, F.: IT project failure rates: facts and reasons. Faeth Choaching, New York (2012). http://faethcoaching.com/it-project-failure-rates-facts-and-reasons/
4. Junior, S.A.S.: Gamificação: Introdução e conceitos básicos (Gamification: An Introduction and Basic Concepts), São Paulo (2014)
5. Schwaber, K.; Sutherland, J.: Guia do Scrum: Um guia definitivo para o Scrum: as regras do jogo (A Guide to Scrum: The Definitive Guide to Scrum: The Rules of the Game) (2011)

Motivating Factors in Agile and Traditional Software Development Methods: A Comparative Study

Regina Albuquerque[1]([⊠]), Rosilene Fernandes[1], Rafaela Mantovani Fontana[2],
Sheila Reinehr[1], and Andreia Malucelli[1]

[1] Pontifical Catholic University of Paraná, PUCPR, R. Imaculada Conceição, 1155,
Curitiba, PR 80215-901, Brazil
{regina.albuquerque,rosilene.fernandes,sheila.reinehr}@pucpr.br,
malu@ppgia.pucpr.br
[2] Federal University of Paraná, UFPR, R. Dr. Alcides Vieira Arcoverde, 1225,
Curitiba, PR 81520-260, Brazil
rafaela.fontana@ufpr.br

Abstract. We here present an investigation into how different software processes may influence software engineers' motivation. For that, we conducted a qualitative cases study comparing motivating factors for individuals who work with a prescriptive (traditional) process with the factors for individuals who work with an adaptive (agile) process. The analysis was based on Alderfer's ERG Theory. Our results show that there are differences in motivating factors, contributing to evidence that work processes do influence the motivation of software engineering practitioners.

Keywords: Software process · Motivation · Agile software development

1 Introduction

A software process defines the steps that should be taken to create the software product, and also influences projects' rhythm and artifacts. While the traditional – or prescriptive – software process focus on up-front planning, using artifacts for documenting the product and formal controlling [3], agile – or adaptive – processes consider source code as the main artifact and value communication and interaction between individuals over comprehensive documentation [2]. Although conciliation between these two approaches is possible [4], the different emphasis given to documentation, communication and planning is evident [1,2].

The premise under this study is that the difference between agile and traditional methods might influence the motivation of the individuals involved. Motivation is one of the human factors recognized as directly influencing project performance and success in software projects [5]. Theoretical and empirical investigation in a number of studies have shown that motivation is dependent on the context and varies from one individual to another [6].

T. Silva da Silva et al. (Eds.): WBMA 2016, CCIS 680, pp. 136–141, 2017.
DOI: 10.1007/978-3-319-55907-0_13

Our objective is thus to understand the motivating factors for software practitioners work in software companies that use two different approaches for producing software: the traditional and the agile software process. The research question that guides us is: *"How does the motivation of traditional software process practitioners differ from the motivation of agile software process practitioners?"*. To answer it, we conducted a qualitative cases study in two organizations. Our results contribute to understanding how software practitioners' motivation is influenced by work processes context.

This paper is organized as follows: the next Section briefly describes studies related to motivation in software engineering; Sect. 3 describes our theoretical foundation; Sect. 4 presents our research approach and Sect. 5 shows our results. Finally, Sect. 6 discusses the results and presents the conclusions.

2   Motivation in Software Engineering

Recent studies have shown that individuals' demotivation to work contributes to project failure [5]. Albeit an important issue, motivation is a complex subject given that motivating factors are diverse and dependent on context and individuals [7]. Beecham et al. [7] have identified that software engineering itself is the main motivator for software engineers, which is complemented by França et al. [6], who identified that clear growth perspectives, clear objectives and team cohesion also motivate software engineers.

Other researches suggest, however, that extrinsic motivators – such as rewards and work conditions and environment – are becoming as important as intrinsic motivators [5,6,8]. For example, Hall et al. [8] identified that good management practices positively influenced developers' performance. The authors identified other extrinsic motivators, such as rewards for appropriate behavior, giving tasks according to people's profiles and a good infrastructure.

In respect to agile methods specifically, Melo et al. [9] identified that there are distinct motivating factors, such as sense of accomplishment, technical challenges at work, good management, feedback, team relationship, experimentation to gain experience and elimination of waste (mainly related to tasks automation).

According to França et al. [6], theoretical and empirical studies indicate that motivation is idiosyncratic to context and varies among practitioners. To contribute to academic studies in the field, we conducted this study presenting motivating factors in a specific context. We founded our analysis on an existing classical motivation theory, as suggested by [7], presented in the next Section.

3   Theoretical Foundation

A number of different theories and approaches have been proposed over the years to explain human being motivation in organizations. Some of them are based on human needs to explain motivational phenomena, such as: Maslow's Hierarchy of Needs, McClelland's Three Needs Theory, McGregor's Theory X and Theory Y, Alderfer's Existence, Relatedness and Growth (ERG) Theory [10] and Herzberg's Two-Factor Theory.

We chose Alderfer's ERG Theory to guide our study because it does not point out dependencies between different types of needs. It allowed us to characterize motivation independently of the satisfaction of other types of needs. According to Alderfer [10], in the organizational environment, a human being has three types of needs to be met: (i) existence, (ii) relatedness, and (iii) growth. Existence need is the most concrete one because it comprises material and physiological desires, such as pay, benefits, infrastructure and work conditions. Relatedness comprehends needs related to interpersonal relationship with superiors, coworkers and subordinates, friends and even enemies. Growth needs "include all the needs which involve a person making creative or productive effects on himself and the environment" [10, p. 146]. Alderfer states that there is no hierarchy in individuals' central needs in the organizational environment. However, if a less concrete need is not met, the desire to meet a more concrete need will grow [10].

These three needs were applied to this study to guide data collection and analysis, as explained in the next Section.

4   Research Approach

We conducted this research as a qualitative case study, according to the guidelines provided by Yin [11]. Our research question was *"How does the motivation of traditional software process practitioners differ from the motivation of agile software process practitioners?"* and was answered by testing three propositions:

- P1 - Existence motivating factors in traditional software development *do not* differ from existence motivating factors in agile software development;
- P2 - Relatedness motivating factors in traditional software development *do not* differ from relatedness motivating factors in agile software development;
- P3 - Growth motivating factors in traditional software development *do not* differ from growth motivating factors in agile software development;

The unit of analysis was the individual – software practitioner – that works with either a traditional or an agile software process. Data was collected by semi-structured interviews, with questions based on the evaluation of the propositions. Each interview took about 30 min. They were all recorded and transcribed for analysis. Six individuals were interviewed. Three of them worked in an organization that used a traditional software process based on Rational Unified Process; and the other three worked in an organization that used Lean as an agile method for software development.

The analysis of the interviews was performed based on the content analysis technique [12]. We analyzed all the transcribed interviews searching for codes related to Alderfer's ERG Theory [10]. A network analysis of codes was created for each ERG category and for each group of interviewees.

5   Results

This section presents the results of the cross-case analysis, when networks of codes were compared between individuals that work with traditional methods and individuals that work with agile methods. Results are described comparatively for each ERG category.

5.1   Existence

In the existence needs category, we could find two subcategories, which group evidences from interviews: *satisfaction of financial needs* and *satisfaction of work conditions*. For the first subcategory, individuals that use both agile and traditional processes showed to be satisfied with salaries and benefits. We found three elements in common among them: (i) their salary is compatible with the market; (ii) there is no reward system related to the method used for software development; and (iii) there is no expectation of salary growth related to the method used for software development.

For the second subcategory – satisfaction of work conditions – we also observed similar evidence in both groups: they feel that the software process organizes the work environment. Yet agile practitioners mentioned that the method (i) allows work to be divided into smaller parts and, as a consequence, results are easier to accomplish; and (ii) individual management of the tasks.

5.2   Relatedness

We found three subcategories comprising the relatedness category: *individual and team, individual and superior*, and *esteem*. For the *individual and team* subcategory, we observed that individuals from both groups consider that the work environment is collaborative, but there are members in the team who seem to feel indifferent as regards the development method used. For traditional process interviewees: (i) people are committed, but (ii) a not-committed team member is a demotivating factor. In the agile process group, we identified that people feel stimulated to work as a team and pointed out that (i) responsibility is shared, (ii) knowledge is shared and (iii) there is a sense of union in the team.

Concerning the *individual and superior* subcategory, we could not find common motivating factors. In the traditional process group, leadership commitment highly influences team members' motivation. We observed that there is an open relationship between individuals and their superiors. For the individuals that use agile methods, leadership commitment seems to have little influence on motivation. Instead, the main motivating factor is collaborative decision making.

The *esteem* subcategory evidences professional appreciation as the main motivator in both groups. For individuals that use traditional methods, we also observed people feeling motivated for (i) being useful in the company; (ii) having a sense of accomplishment by working on innovative projects; and (iii) meeting customers' expectations. In the agile process group we identified the sense of self-assertion in the team.

5.3 Growth

According to Alderfer [10], satisfaction with growth needs happen when people are challenged to solve problems that fully apply their capabilities and make them develop new skills. For to this category, we found that learning is a common motivating factor in both groups. Interviewees feel motivated to learn and to apply new methodologies in their work activities.

For the group that uses the traditional process, we observed that motivation is met when people are challenged to solve problems, to execute innovative projects and meet customers' expectations. We found other factors for the individuals that use an agile process: (i) the development of an individual accountability, considering that responsibility is shared among the team; (ii) the prestige in software development market – according to interviewees, working with agile method enriches employability; (iii) using agile methods for solving personal problems; and, finally (iv) autonomy to be creative to solve problems.

6 Discussion and Conclusions

The results presented in the previous Section allow us to answer our research question by confirming that motivating factors do *differ* – under some aspects – between individuals that work with a traditional software development method and individuals that work with an agile software development method.

Recalling our study propositions, we observe that *P1 was confirmed*, and propositions *P2 and P3 were not confirmed*. We verified that, regarding existence aspects, motivating factors are similar among traditional and agile groups. Concerning relatedness and growth, motivating factors were different between them.

Regarding existence, we observed that most motivating factors are present in both groups. The only difference appears when agile practitioners mention that they value the individual management of their tasks, which is a characteristic of the method they use. In the relatedness category, a number of differences were found. We observed that leadership commitment has a stronger influence on motivation when people work with traditional processes. In this group, we also found out that demotivated individuals badly influence other team members' motivation. For agile practitioners, we did not identify this influence. Esteem also differs between the groups. While in the traditional process we observed motivation when people feel useful at work, in the agile process, people feel motivated by self-assertion in the team. In the growth category, differences were also observed mainly for the fact that, in traditional processes, motivation is related to meeting customers' expectation and professional challenge. For agile processes, growth motivation relates to individual accountability and autonomy.

When comparing our results to the existing literature, we observe that some motivating factors were confirmed. Considering the traditional software process, we observed similarities regarding the relatedness category: leader's influence on motivation, good relationship with team members and superiors, collaborative and team work were factors also identified in [5,6,8]. Concerning the agile software process, we confirmed some factors identified in [9]: the sense of accomplishment, feedback and involvement with the team. Besides, we identified that learning and professional challenge are motivating factors for people who work with either software process, which confirms Beecham et al.'s [7] statement that software engineers get motivated by software engineering itself.

Although our results contribute to expanding the literature regarding human aspects in software engineering and to managers concerned in motivating their teams, we considered they are limited for (i) the sample size and (ii) the organizational contexts in which the research was conducted. Data obtained from the six interviews might prevent results generalization and raises the need for confirmatory studies. As we performed case studies in two different organizations, the organizational context might also have influenced the motivating factors described by interviewees. We thus plan to conduct future studies in a single organization that uses both traditional and agile software process models.

References

1. Germain, E., Robillard, P.N.: Engineering-based process and agile methodologies for software development: a comparative case study. J. Syst. Softw. **75**, 17–27 (2005). doi:10.1016/j.jss.2004.02.022
2. Beck, K., et al.: Manifesto for agile software development (2001). http://www.agilemanifesto.org
3. Kroll, P., Hrutchen, P.: The Rational Unified Process Made Easy: A Practitioners Guide to the RUP. Pearson Education, Boston (2003)
4. Magdaleno, A.M., Werner, C.M., Araujo, R.M.: Reconciling software development models: a quasi-systematic review. J. Syst. Softw. **85**, 351–369 (2012). doi:10.1016/j.jss.2011.08.028
5. Verner, J.M., Babar, M.A., Cerpa, N., Hall, T., Beecham, S.: Factors that motivate software engineering teams: a four country empirical study. J. Syst. Softw. **92**, 115–127 (2014). doi:10.1016/j.jss.2014.01.008
6. França, C., Silva, F.Q., Feliz, A.L.C., Carneiro, D.E.S.: Motivation in software engineering practice: a cross-case analysis of two software organisations. Inf. Softw. Tech. **56**, 79–101 (2014). doi:10.1016/j.infsof.2013.06.006
7. Beecham, S., Baddoo, N., Hall, T., Robinson, H., Sharp, H.: Motivation in software engineering: a systematic literature review. Inf. Softw. Tech. **50**, 860–878 (2008). doi:10.1016/j.infsof.2007.09.004
8. Hall, T., Jagilska, D., Baddoo, N.: Motivating developer performance to improve project outcomes in a high maturity organization. Softw. Qual. J. **15**, 365–381 (2007). doi:10.1007/s11219-007-9028-1
9. Melo, C.O., Santana, C., Kon, F.: Developers motivation in agile teams. In: 38th Euromicro Conference on Software Engineering and Advanced Applications (2012). doi:10.1109/SEAA.2012.45
10. Alderfer, C.P.: An empirical test of a new theory of human needs. Organ. Behav. Hum. Perf. **4**(2), 142–175 (1969). doi:10.1016/0030-5073(69)90004-X
11. Yin, R.K.: Case Study Research: Design and Methods, 5th edn. Sage Publications, Thousand Oaks (2013)
12. Bardin, L.: Análise de Conteúdo. Edições 70, Lisboa (2011)

Quality Assurance in Agile Software Development: A Systematic Review

Carlos Alberto Fortunato[1(✉)], Felipe Furtado[1], Fernando Selleri[2],
Ivaldir de Farias Junior[3], and Nelson Leitão Júnior[1]

[1] CESAR.EDU, Recife, PE, Brasil
calbertofortunato@gmail.com, furtado.fs@gmail.com,
leitaojr@outlook.com
[2] UNEMAT - Universidade do Estado do Mato Grosso,
Barra do Bugres, MT, Brasil
selleri@unemat.br
[3] Softex Recife, Recife, PE, Brasil
ivaldirjr@gmail.com

Abstract. In software engineering, agile methods have emerged as alternative to handle the growing pressures for innovation in increasingly shorter deadlines, the constant needs for changes in requirements and the poor performance of most software development projects accelerating time to market, bring improvements in quality and productivity, Information Technology (IT)/business alignment, and enhanced flexibility are noticed. In this context, through a systematic literature review, this work aims to identify, evaluate and analyze relevant studies on quality assurance practices in agile. The results include the identified works, practices and limitations.

Keywords: Agile software development · Quality assurance · Agile practices

1 Introduction

Software development using agile methods have been increasingly used by the software development industry. When compared to traditional software development methods, advantages such as accelerate time to market, increase in quality and productivity, improve Information Technology (IT)/business alignment, and enhanced flexibility are noticed [1]. In order to contribute to the improvement of process and product quality, this work aims to identify the quality assurance practices that are present in agile software development.

2 Methodology Approach

As stated by Kitchenham and Charters [2], a systematic literature review aims to assess, identify and support all relevant studies available for a specific research question, subject area, or phenomenon of interest. This section presents the research protocol used in this study, having as reference the studies described by Dyba and Dingsøyr [3] and Selleri et al. [4].

© Springer International Publishing AG 2017
T. Silva da Silva et al. (Eds.): WBMA 2016, CCIS 680, pp. 142–148, 2017.
DOI: 10.1007/978-3-319-55907-0_14

2.1   Research Questions

This study aims to answer the following research questions (RQ): (RQ1) which practices are used for quality assurance in agile projects? (RQ2) What are the main challenges and limitations of quality assurance on agile methods?

2.2   Data Sources and Search Terms

Based on Selleri et al. (2014), the research protocol of this paper adopts manual and automated database searches. The ACM Digital Library, IEEE Explorer, Science Direct, Scopus, Springerlink, Wiley Inter Science Journal Finder where used as indexation mechanisms. For manual searches, the following conferences were selected: XP Conference; Agile Development Conference; International Conference on the Quality of Information and Communications Technology; International Conference on Software Engineering Advances; International Symposium on Empirical Software Engineering and Measurement; International Conference on Software Engineering. The following journals were selected: IEEE Transactions on Software Engineering; Journal of the ACM; ACM Transactions on Software Engineering and Methodology; IEEE Software; Empirical Software Engineering Journal; Journal of Software Process: Improvement and Practice; Agile Journal.

The search in the electronic databases used keywords derived from the previous research such Dyba and Dingsøyr [3] and Selleri et al [4]. By combining these terms with the logical operators AND and OR, we obtained the following search string: ("*Quality Assurance*" OR "SQA" OR "QA") AND ("*agile*" OR "*agility*" OR "*lightweight*" OR "*scrum*" OR "*extreme programming*" OR "XP" OR "*dynamic system development*" OR "DSDM" OR "*crystal clear*" OR "*crystal orange*" OR "*crystal red*" OR "*crystal blue*" OR "*feature driven development*" OR "FDD" OR "*lean software development*" OR "*adaptive software development*" OR "ASD" OR "*test driven development*" OR "TDD").

2.3   Criteria and Procedures for Studies Selection

We adopted the following criteria for studies inclusion: academic and industry studies with empirical data; works from conference and journals; experience reports on quality assurance in agile development; studies in English; studies published between 2001 and 2015; qualitative or quantitative research studies. The following criteria were adopted to studies exclusion: studies without the focus on quality assurance and agile development; editorials, prefaces, article summaries, interviews, news, analysis, correspondence, discussions, comments, reader letters, tutorials, summaries, workshops' plan, panels and poster sessions; studies that focus on simple techniques or practices.

The selection of primary studies was carried out in four stages, by applying the inclusion and exclusion criteria adopted in Selleri et al. [4], they are: Step 1: automatic search and manual search (duplicate studies were discarded); Step 2: identification of potentially relevant studies by analysis of the title and abstract, discarding clearly irrelevant studies for research; Step 3: a review of studies by reading the introduction, methodology, results, considerations, and if necessary throughout the text; Step 4: critical reading of articles, including checking of references to obtain further study.

2.4   Performing the Review

The review began with the automatic search through the search string in the defined mechanisms and the manual search. It was followed by the identification of potentially relevant studies and the application of the inclusion/exclusion criteria. We identified 2992 papers, which are distributed by electronic databases as follows: IEEE (95), Wiley Inter Science Journal Finder (191), ACM Digital Library (244), Springer Link (311), Science Direct (710) and Scopus (1441). For manual search, we identified 12 works in this disposition: QUATIC (1), Agile Conference (2), ICSEA (2), ICSE (3), XP Conference (4). The results of the automatic search (2992) and manual search (12) were consolidated in 3004 results. The studies were ordered by title to the exclusion of redundancies, resulting in 2,950 studies. The studies that did not have to mention quality assurance using agile practices in the title or abstract were discarded, elapsing 304 studies. Then the reference lists of included studies were checked, which led to 8 studies, bringing the total to 312 studies, which were read. Then, were excluded those which did not identify the use of practices common to agile methods or did not refer to the product and process quality gain from its use and were included 3 of 8 studies identified by the review of references, totaling 22 studies.

3   Results

The 22 identified studies, available in following link (https://goo.gl/nJcc0U), led to the following results.

3.1   Agile Practices

Figure 1 shows the agile practices identified in the analyzed studies.

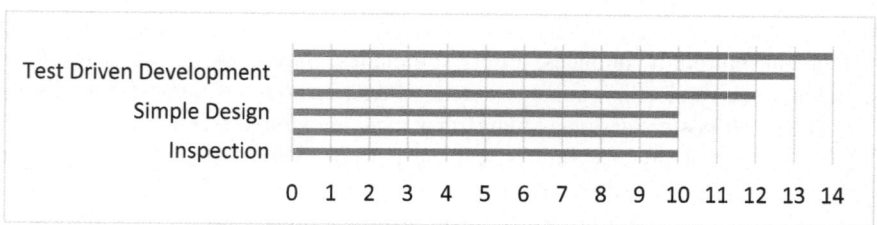

Fig. 1. Agile practices identified in the works

The most cited practices in the works are part of the Extreme Programming methodology, as being the "Refactoring" the most used practice that was present in fourteen works. Secondly, the practice of "Testing Driven Development" being present in thirteen works. The "Knowledge Sharing" practice was identified in twelve works and the "Pair Programming", "Inspection" and "Simple Design" practices were present in ten works. The "System Metaphor" and "Continuous Integration", were both in nine works. Scrum Practices, as the "Retrospective", "Stand-up Meetings", "Sprint Review" and "Planning" meetings, were mentioned in six works and these were mentioned as favoring quality assurance. Agile practices related to FDD such "Domain Object Modeling"; "Feature Teams" and "Progress Reporting"; and Crystal Clear such "Joint Planning Meeting" were cited at least in one of the included studies.

3.2 Quality Assurance in Agile Methods

Answering the question (Q1) of this study, Table 1 shows the works and their respective practices that enable quality assurance in agile methods. Each study was identified by a prefix "s" to "study" and a sequence indicator, both in parenthesis.

Table 1. Work and related practices

Work	Related practices
(s1)	The study was based on 10 projects identified gain quality with the use of agile practices such as test-driven development, refactoring, pair programming, and recruiting people with good technical level and ongoing communication with the customer.
(s2)	The study identified the practices that leverage quality projects that make use of Scrum as validation of user stories; multidisciplinary team; software construction with parallel tests; continuous improvement of technical knowledge of the team; test automation; advanced use pair programming and review.
(s3)	The study was based on 42 institutions, and identified gain in quality as the use of practices such as continuous customer communication, knowledge sharing, small teams, well organized and trained, flexible code design and refactoring code and database.
(s4), (s5), (s13)	The studies identified the main agile practices derived from XP favoring quality assurance: development guided by tests; refactoring; system metaphor and pair programming.
(s5)	The study identified the use of the quality manager and the creation of a contingency plan for major mishaps during the software lifecycle promote the quality of the final product.
(s6)	The study identified the practices that promote quality assurance as refactoring, continuous integration, making smaller deliveries, code review, pair programming and testing.

(continued)

Table 1. (*continued*)

Work	Related practices
(s7)	The study proposed a model called Agile Quality Assurance Model (AQAM), where the main focus is on quality assurance in agile management, some key areas in the development process are based on agile practices such as pair programming, sharing knowledge, unit testing and continuous integration.
(s8)	The study describes XP practices such as those focused on risk control and quality of code produced, rather than relying on a process that will only check the quality of the final product, as follows: System metaphor, customer presence at the developers, and improvement in communication between members of the team, pair programming, refactoring, continuous feedback and acceptance testing.
(s9)	The study proposes the scope of the ISO 9126 quality attributes (Correctness, Maintainability, verifiability, efficiency, availability, portability, testability and reliability) through agile practices derived from XP.
(s10)	The study identified the practices responsible for quality assurance: test driven development, acceptance testing, code inspection, pair programming, refactoring, continuous integration, collaborative work, system metaphor, continuous feedback and coding best practices.
(s11)	The study mentioned test driven development and acceptance testing as agile practices that promoting quality assurance.
(s12)	The study proposes the so-called Continuous Integration, Continuous Measurement and Continuous Improvement (3C) in which quality assurance is achieved from an improvement of the practice of Continuous Integration.
(s13), (s19)	The studies claim that the practices of Scrum and XP, as the daily meeting, acceptance testing and continuous integration allow quality assurance in agile process and not allow changes while Sprint prevents the uncontrolled growth of the project scope.
(s14)	The study made a comparison between XP and Waterfall model, in which were identified the following practices that enable quality assurance: pair programming, refactoring, system metaphor, on-site customer with the team, constant feedback, unit testing and acceptance, development team with people who together take responsibility for ensuring the project, focusing on collaborative work, interpersonal constant improvement and motivation.
(s15)	The study identified some practices that promote quality assurance in the Scrum framework and continuous collaboration, integration testing, continuous feedback and development, knowledge sharing, retrospective, and daily meetings.
(s4), (s16)	Both said that the test application in all stages of development enables error detection during the iterations of the software life cycle, adding the use of refactoring, applied correctly, which increases the architectural quality and the convenience of maintenance code for future iterations. Also with the improvement in communication, disseminating knowledge about the problems and methods to solve them, then identifies the possibility of quality assurance.

(*continued*)

Table 1. (*continued*)

Work	Related practices
(s18)	The study mapped out a set of practices necessary to reach some quality attributes defined by ISO 9126, which are: unit testing, retrospective, pair programming and inspection.
(s18), (s21)	The studies identified for Crystal Clear methodology, practices such as test automation, direct involvement of the user and revisions enable quality assurance.
(s21)	The study evaluated six methods from the framework perspective "good enough quality" and identified the following practices as quality assurance enablers: software demonstration, joint planning meeting, joint application development, customer on-site prototyping, automated acceptance testing, continuous integration testing, inspection, pair programming, test driven development, coding and refactoring patterns.
(s17), (s20), (s22)	The mapped practices from Scrum and XP such system metaphor, on-site customer with the team, constant feedback, unit and acceptance testing, continuous integration, coding and refactoring patterns, pair programming, stand up meting enable quality assurance.

3.3 Challenges and Limitations for the Quality Assurance in Agile Methods

In response to the research question (Q2) of this work, Table 2 shows the works with their limitations and challenges related to quality assurance in agile methods.

Table 2. Works and their related limitations and challenges

Works	Related limitations and challenges
(s11)	The study proposes that should be avoided the developer testing as the sole approach, because you cannot make use of destructive attitudes when planning the tests.
(s19)	The study states that the productivity and quality printed by the Scrum agile methodology is closely related to the talent and expertise of the team; the lack of a consolidated guide practices on the implementation of testing and dependence on interpersonal talent team directly impact the quality of the final product.
(s21)	The study states that empirical studies did not show an improvement in quality from the customer's use at the team of developers, which may not have the skills to take on this important role, which strengthened the guarantee of the quality of the final product.
(s22)	The study exposes the limitations in identifying bugs by using unit tests for a lot of code, because the degree of coverage tests in relation to the vast number of possible scenarios may be insufficient.

4 Final Remarks and Future Work

From the reading and extraction of data on ensuring agile quality, we identified that the use of people with a generalist professional profile, who treat teamwork and good communication between team members as a philosophy, which are adept of constant knowledge improvement and favor the perfectionism, support the adoption of agile methods in projects, as corroborated by the latest Chaos Report [5], that states that one of the factors that contributed to the success of the projects were the use of proficient agile people. Also, as stated by analyzed works, the use of good programming practices is regarded as one of the pillars of quality assurance, making the training and retraining of the team in techniques such as coding standards, refactoring, creating unit tests, review code, pair programming and use of continuous integration tools are important factors for achieving the quality assurance. Regarding the identified limitations on agile practices, software testing proved as the most likely to be incorrectly performed, but, as stated by VersionOne [6], one of the main challenges in agile projects it is the lack of knowledge of agile practices. It should also be noticed that the work (s18) mentions some quality attributes such as reusability, portability and compatibility (ISO 9126) by only linking their role in quality maintenance with object-oriented languages, as well as the work (s11), that does not mention the use of testers for supporting the developers in the creation of destructive test scenarios that will be covered by unit tests. Works from Brazil relating quality assurance and agile practices were not found in the period searched (2001 to 2015). As future work, we suggest the proposition of a model that qualify and quantify the use of practices that make up the agile ecosystem, to achieve the final product quality attributes proposed in ISO 9126 [7].

References

1. Campanelli, A.S., Parreiras, F.S.: Agile methods tailoring - a systematic literature review. J. Syst. Softw. **110**, 85–100 (2015)
2. Kitchenham, B., Charters, S.: Guidelines for performing systematic literature reviews in software engineering. Technical report, School of Computer Science and Mathematics, Keele University (2007)
3. Dybå, T., Dingsøyr, T.: Empirical studies of agile software development: a systematic review. Inf. Softw. Technol. **50**, 833–859 (2008)
4. Selleri, F., Furtado, F.S.S., Peres, A.L., Azevedo, I.M., Vasconcelos, A.P., Kamei, F.K., Meira, S.R.L.: Using CMMI together with agile software development: a systematic review. Inf. Softw. Technol. **58**, 20–43 (2014). doi:10.1016/j.infsof.2014.09.012. Elsevier Editorial System(tm)
5. Standish Group: The Chaos Report (2015). http://www.standishgroup.com
6. VersionOne: State of Agile Development Survey Results (2015). http://www.versionone.com
7. ISO/IEC 9126. Software Engineer Standard (2003). http://www.iso.org/

Author Index